BRITAIN IN OLD PHOTOGRAPHS

BRISLINGTON REVISITED

GRAHAM CRIMMINS, LYNDA HARRIS,
BETH KNIGHT AND JONATHAN ROWE

ACKNOWLEDGEMENTS

Brislington Conservation and History Society wishes to thank the following people for help with information and loan, donation and copying of photographs: Rosalind Anstey, *Bristol Evening Post*, Margaret Bryant, Janice Coggins, Graham and Joan Crimmins, Edwin Clark, Marie Clark, Elizabeth Clark, Peter Davey Tram Collection, Pete Evans, Lynda Harris, Pat Hase, Delphine Higgs, Mike Hooper, Phil and Beth Knight, Dennis Lukins, J. Merrett, David Napier, Friends of Arnos Vale Cemetery, Peggy Poole, Jonathan Rowe, St Anne's Church archive, St Cuthbert's Church archive, Sid Spiers, Colin Tarr, Bob Thomas, Mike Tozer Collection, Colston West, Bryan Wilson.

Apologies to photograph owners or anyone omitted from the above list.

First published 2008

The History Press Ltd.
The Mill, Brimscombe Port
Stroud, Gloucestershire, GL5 2QG
www.thehistorypress.co.uk

Reprinted 2009, 2014

© Graham Crimmins, Lynda Harris, Beth Knight and Jonathan Rowe, 2008

The right of Graham Crimmins, Lynda Harris, Beth Knight
and Jonathan Rowe to be identified as the Authors
of this work has been asserted in accordance with the
Copyrights, Designs and Patents Act 1988.

All rights reserved. No part of this book may be reprinted
or reproduced or utilised in any form or by any electronic,
mechanical or other means, now known or hereafter invented,
including photocopying and recording, or in any information
storage or retrieval system, without the permission in writing
from the Publishers.
British Library Cataloguing in Publication Data.
A catalogue record for this book is available from the British Library.

ISBN 978 0 7524 4555 7

Typesetting and origination by The History Press Ltd.
Printed in Great Britain

CONTENTS

	Acknowledgements	2
	Introduction	5
1	Victoria to the Great War 1880–1918	7
2	The Roaring Twenties 1919–1929	27
3	Brislington into Bristol 1930–1939	39
4	War and Austerity 1940–1949	53
5	You've Never Had It So Good 1950–1959	65
6	The Swinging Sixties 1960–1969	77
7	Recession and Redevelopment 1970 to the Present Day	97

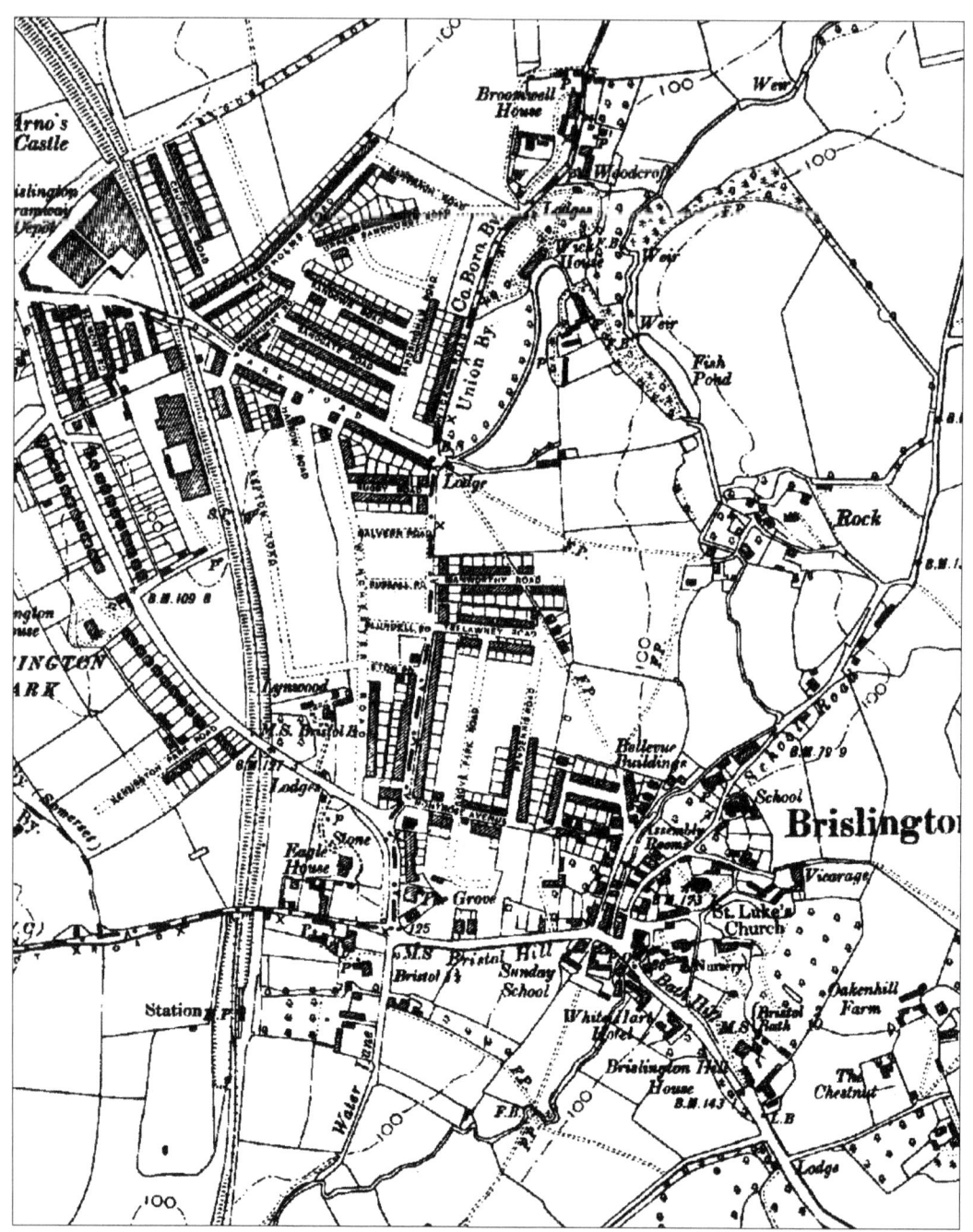

Map of Brislington, *c.* 1900.

INTRODUCTION

The history of Brislington stretches from prehistory and Romano-British times, through to the days of pilgrims visiting the Chapel of St Anne in the Wood and the Holy Well. For many years it remained a small rural village on the route from Bristol to Bath which during the eighteenth century became the seat of the local gentry and favoured retreat of Bristol merchants who had 'got up in the world'.[1] In the twentieth century it succumbed to urbanisation and industrial development as a suburb on the outskirts of Bristol.

The old parish of Brislington, illustrated on the 1846 Tithe Map, took in not only the present village, Sandy Park, St Anne's and Broomhill areas, but also parts of what are now Hengrove and Knowle West. It was bordered by no fewer than seven other parishes – Bedminster, Whitchurch, Hanham, Keynsham, St Philip, St Jacob and St George. The village came within the compass of the Bristol city boundary in 1933, and currently comprises the two wards of Brislington East and West, with a population of approx 25,000.

This book is the second volume produced by the Brislington Conservation and History Society, the first having been published in 1995. The society was invited to produce a second book and we were pleased to be able to compile this publication in time to mark the twenty-fifth anniversary of its formation in 1984. The society was established to promote local history research, conservation of both buildings and natural habitat, and to prevent unsympathetic development in Brislington. At the beginning of the twentieth century, Brislington had been a rural country community, once called the prettiest village in Somerset, but by the late twentieth century it was a built-up suburb of Bristol.

The idea of a society to record and protect the area's past and to try to safeguard its future, was born at a meeting in the home of Martin Lee, a teacher at Brislington School and a member of Bristol Civic Society. The meeting was attended by Dorothy Brown, Chairman of Bristol Visual and Environmental Group, who was later awarded an MBE for her work in the area of conservation. Also present were father and son, Norman and Jonathan Rowe, who were to become prominent members of the society. Norman was a printer at John Wright's in Brislington and a former Bristol City councillor, a school governor and trade unionist who was very active in local politics and in the life of the village church of St Luke. He became the vice-chairman of the society, a post he held for about fifteen years until ill health forced his retirement. Jonathan, an amateur

---

[1] Presbyterian Minister, Revd Joseph Hunter from Bath, visited George Weare Braikenridge at Broomwell House, Brislington, in 1830 and wrote: 'For his own village, Brislington, he (Braikenridge) has had a large collection of drawings made ... at great expense: so as to preserve a complete impression of what Brislington now is, the favourite retreat of Bristol merchants when got up in the world.'

local historian, is also secretary of St Luke's Church Players and writes original material for productions. He became the chairman of the society in 2005.

Following the initial meeting, a public event was held in St Luke's Church Hall attended by approximately 200 people. After a second meeting a constitution was formed and the society was launched as the Brislington Conservation and Amenity Society, the name it held until 2003. The first chairman was Bobbie Frankham, an accountant who grew up in Brislington. After the untimely death of the first secretary, June McCarthy, this post was taken up by Mary Mitchell, who later combined the roles of secretary and chairman for many years until her retirement in 2005. Altogether she gave nearly twenty years' service to the society, the executive committee meetings being held in her seventeenth-century home, Keeper's Cottage, on Brislington Hill.

The society originally had three groups to oversee local history research; current and future development; and conservation. These were led respectively by Jonathan Rowe, Norman Rowe and Sam Wyatt, the latter being a former city councillor and a well-known architect whose name is perpetuated in Wyatt's View, a road on the former St Anne's Board Mills redevelopment.

In the early years of the society, a Brislington Conservation Area was created, centred on what remained of the old village. The society became deeply involved in saving the historic Victorian house, Lynwood, on the Bath Road, which was preserved from the threat of demolition and became a Listed building. Latterly, we have also helped with listing a summerhouse originally belonging to Wick House, one of Brislington's great houses.

Over the last twenty-five years, hundreds of talks, slide evenings, guided walks, visits and exhibitions have been held and many local history leaflets have been written, including an occasional series of local history pamphlets, the *Brislington Bugle*. The society has also collaborated in the making and issue of two DVDs, *Yesterday's Brislington* (2001) and *Brislington Remembered* (2002).

To the present day, the society continues to monitor planning applications and makes representations where proposals are deemed to be detrimental to the local area. It is encouraging to note that local primary schools continue to teach pupils about the history in their area. This includes taking the children on walks around the neighbourhood, many of which are conducted by the society's vice-chairman, Janice Coggins, whose family has a long association with Brislington.

As a group, Brislington Conservation and History Society has sought to record and preserve Brislington's rich heritage for future generations, to raise public awareness of the area's fascinating past as well as stimulate interest in Brislington today and ongoing issues which affect its future. The majority of the photographs in this book have never been published before, and we hope that *Brislington Revisited*, part of the *Britain in Old Photographs* series, will give readers a view of what Brislington once was, as well as being a nostalgic look back at days gone by.

1

VICTORIA TO THE GREAT WAR 1880–1918

The village smithy, Brislington Village, *c.* 1890.

In 1878, when Queen Victoria had been on the throne for forty-one years, Brislington acquired its first purpose-built 'town houses' in Bellevue Park and Bellevue Terrace. These were followed in the early 1880s by large Victorian villas in Kensington Hill on the Bath Road, and in the 1890s by rather less grand rows of terraced housing which started to spring up in the Sandy Park area. At the same time, the development of St Anne's, known as 'New Brislington', began on the former Langton Court Estate. In the early years of the twentieth century, more of the grounds belonging to old estates were built on, notably The Grove in Wick Road, which became Grove Park Road, Grove Park Avenue, Pendennis Park, Montrose Park, Trelawney Park and Bristol Hill. Fortunately, The Grove itself is one of the old houses which still remains, albeit long since converted into flats.

The spiritual needs of the expanding population were served by a range of religious dominations. The fifteenth-century parish church of St Luke was altered and lengthened in 1874 and the churchyard was extended the following year when the old village lock-up was demolished. In 1878 Brislington's first public meeting hall, the Band of Hope Assembly Rooms (now the Christadelphian Church) was opened. A Wesleyan Methodist church was built in the village in 1885 and a new Congregational church (now the United Reformed church) appeared at the end of Wick Road in 1901. The St Anne's area was not left out – a corrugated-iron mission church was erected in 1896, later replaced by the present building in Salisbury Road which was completed in 1909. The original 'tin church' moved to the top of Allison Road/Sandy Park Road, and became the St Cuthbert's Mission Church in 1906.

The church also provided the first education for children based initially on three sites from 1822, then combined into one school in 1859 in School Road. By the turn of the century, the increase in population required new schools to be built to accommodate the growing number of children – St Anne's (1900), Wick Road (1905) and Hollywood Road (1913) which catered for infants, juniors and senior boys and girls. Separate blocks were provided for each age range, which are still recorded in the names over the entrance doors.

Brislington Tramway Depot was built in 1899 and the next year the tram line was extended right into the village. Motor cars were first seen around 1903 and in 1913 the cinema arrived with the opening of the Empress (later the Brislington) at the bottom end of Sandy Park Road. Brislington also had its own manual telephone exchange at No. 4 Wick Road in 1906. Modern industry began in 1902 with the opening of Terrell's Rope Works at Arno's Vale, followed by the CWS Butter Factory in Whitby Road in 1904.

Despite these changes, the area around the old village continued to live under the almost feudal yet benevolent regime of 'Squire and Spire', with daily living overseen by local gentry and the Church. These wealthy families (the Clayfield-Irelands and the Cooke-Hurles) had been the major landowners in the village since the late eighteenth century, but their days were numbered, and by the end of the 1920s both had left the area. Nevertheless, Brislington retained its rural atmosphere well into the twentieth century with a dozen working farms and market gardens, a few of which survived into the 1950s.

Broomhill Lane (now Broomhill Road) in the 1880s. This evocative rural view of Brislington around 120 years ago would still have been recognisable well into the first decades of the twentieth century, when there were fields and farmland stretching from what is now Victory Park all the way to Keynsham. The sun-bonneted old lady and the children could have stepped from the pages of a Thomas Hardy novel. What is now the Broomhill area was formerly known to locals as 'Brummel' and this name has lingered in living memory. Broomhill was originally several acres of open fields and agricultural land where skylarks could be seen and heard flying overhead every summer, and it was a favourite secluded spot for local courting couples. Following the discovery of an oak box containing horseshoe nails, identified as being similar to those used during the English Civil War (1642–1645), it was suggested that Cromwell's troops may have made camp on this hilltop before their attack on Bristol in 1645. Until the 1930s the seventeenth-century Eastwood Farm, which still stands off the present-day Wyndham Crescent, was the only habitation in Broomhill and it remained a working farm until 1959. Modern development began with bungalows built in Broomhill Road in the early 1930s and the area quickly became covered with houses and shops, many of the new roads having Channel Islands' associations; for example Jersey Avenue, Guernsey Avenue and so on.

Interior of the Bath House near Arno's Castle, Bath Road (now the Black Castle) when it was an antique showroom (1911–1918), showing the covered plunge pool. The Bath House was built by a Quaker copper smelter, William Reeve, around 1765 with a passage under the A4 Bath Road from Reeve's Gothic Mansion, Arno's Court. In 1911 the Bath Road was widened and the passage was filled in. The Bath House consisted of a cold bath, a dressing room, a conservatory, and a pinery which supplied pineapples for the Coronation breakfast of Charles X of France, last of the Bourbon kings of France (1824–1830), which took place on 28 May 1825. By the 1930s, the Bath House had become derelict and, following further air-raid damage during the Second World War, it was demolished in 1965. The front colonnade, however, was dismantled in 1957 by Sir Clough Williams-Ellis (1883–1978) and rebuilt at Portmerion, North Wales, where it was officially reopened in April 1959 by Sir Bertrand Russell, and can still be seen today. Williams-Ellis was a campaigner for the environment and a founder member of the Preservation of Rural England (now Campaign to Protect Rural England). The colonnade later achieved further fame when it was seen on television when Portmerion was used as a location for filming the cult 1967 series *The Prisoner*.

Opposite above: Interior of Brislington Congregational Chapel in Holymead Fields (now Kenneth Road area) *c.* 1900. The earliest chapel on this site was established in a barn in 1796 on the large open space known as Holymead Fields, where medieval pilgrims were said to have gathered on the last stage of their journey to St Anne's Chapel in the Wood. A new Congregational chapel was built in 1827 but this was burnt down and rebuilt in 1894. This building was replaced by the new chapel (now Brislington United Reformed Church) on the corner of Wick Road in 1901. The old chapel was later used by Brislington Women's Institute, and later as a skittle alley for the adjacent Hollybush pub, both of which were demolished in 2007 to build Chapel Court flats.

Opposite below: St Luke's Church Choir around 1918 in the garden of the vicarage (Church Hill House, which was the vicarage from 1896–1981) in Church Hill. The man in the centre with dark moustache is Charlie Inman, who was the church organist and choir master from approximately 1913 to 1937.

Brook House in School Road, *c.* 1900. This cottage stood near the site of Castlegate House flats (built 1964), and was demolished around 1950 after being damaged in a wartime air raid. Holly Cottage (No. 100A School Road) can be seen on far left.

School Place and Step House on far right, in School Road, *c.* 1910. Demolished for Nos 136–154 School Road in the 1950s.

Nightingale Valley, c. 1910. St Anne's Terrace on right was built around 1897. Oak Cottage and Elm Cottage on far left date from about 1860. Nightingale Valley became public open space in 1947.

St Anne's Post Office, No. 22 Langton Court Road, St Anne's, c. 1908. St Anne's Post Office was run by the Coe family from approximately 1905 to 1937. Edith Coe was running a draper's shop there in 1901, and continued to sell a variety of merchandise after the shop become a post office, including bicycles, and other items which could be paid for weekly. Very few people had telephones at this time and customers were able to make calls from a pay phone just inside the side door. The post office closed in June 2003.

Left: Dame Eva Turner (1892–1990). The photograph shows her in her most famous role, *Turandot*, which she first sang in 1926. The Puccini opera includes the well-known tenor aria, *Nessun Dorma*.

Below: Blue plaque on St Anne's Schools, corner of Langton Court Road and Bloomfield Road, erected in 2001 to commemorate former pupil, Dame Eva Turner.

Newbridge Road, *c.* 1916. Dame Eva Turner was the first famous English female opera singer and was made a dame in 1962. As a child she lived at Tortworth (No. 184 Newbridge Road) in St Anne's from 1905–1908. The family had moved to Bristol from Oldham, Lancashire in 1902, and previously lived at No. 29 Arlington Road. Eva's father, Charles Turner, was head engineer at the Great Western Cotton Co. at Barton Hill. She attended St Anne's School, and returned there for the Diamond Jubilee celebrations in 1960 when she presented the school with a bell which is still in use today.

ARTHUR E. LANSDOWN,
FAMILY GROCER & PROVISION MERCHANT,

Montrose Avenue Supply Stores, BRISLINGTON.

Noted House for MILD HOME-CURED ENGLISH BACON.   Families waited upon for Orders daily.

Personal Attention.   *Prompt Delivery.*   *Stores Prices.*

Specially appointed Agent for SUPERB "G.P. GOVERNMENT' TEA.

TOM FULLER,
Dairyman,

LINTON FARM, BRISLINGTON

Pure Warm Milk supplied Twice Daily.
Fresh Cream, Butter, New Laid Eggs, Poultry, &c.
All Milk delivered from our own and local Farms.

A. HATHERELL,
Grocer & Provision Merchant.

Noted for the old-fashion Straw-burnt English Bacon.
Noted for Quality and Cheapness.
Our Motto is: "VALUE FOR CASH."
Try our Special Blend of Tea, 1/4, 1/6 and 1/8.
Note the only address:

12 Trelawney Road, Brislington.

Sole Agent for Ward's Vegetable & Flower Seeds.

E. G. RUDGE,
Newsagent, Stationer and Confectioner,
THE PARADE,
ARNO'S VALE, BRISTOL.

Newspapers, Periodicals, &c., delivered daily.
Picture Post Cards a Speciality.

W. PHILLIPS & SON,
Practical Boot and Shoe Makers,
Grove Road, BRISLINGTON.
(Near Pilgrim P.H.)
Hand-sewn, Machine-sewn and Rivet Boots made to order at moderate prices.

Gents' Soled and Heeled from 2/6.
Ladies'   do.   from 1/6.
Children's   do.   from 1/-.

J. VEAL,
Painter, Paperhanger, and House Decorator,

97 WICK ROAD, BRISLINGTON.

GENERAL REPAIRS.   ESTIMATES FREE.

J. ROBERTS,
Earthenware, China and Hardware Merchant,

43 SANDY PARK ROAD.

Noted for Brushes, Brooms and Mats.
LAMPS   Incandescent Mantles and
in great variety.   Fittings.

A. PALMER,
Greengrocer & Fruiterer,

Bottom of **MONTROSE AVENUE, BRISLINGTON.**

Reasonable Prices.   *Fresh Fish Daily.*
TRAPPED RABBITS IN SEASON.

A. M. PROSSER,
Sandy Park Road.

PLUMBER, GAS & HOT WATER FITTER.

ELECTRIC BELLS FITTED.
Repairs of all kinds promptly attended to.

TRY H. CAREY'S
Specially Selected   **TEA & COFFEE.**

Agent for all the leading Tea Houses in the United Kingdom.
Also ESTATE AGENT, Houses to be Let or Sold
(Rents collected at Moderate Terms).
Representative for the London & Lancashire Fire & Life Offices
Also Agent for   COMMISSION AGENT.
The Great Western and General Insurance Company.

Note the Address: **44 Grove Park Avenue, BRISLINGTON.**

M. ASTLEY,
GROVE PARK DAIRY,

GROVE PARK ROAD.
Brislington, Bristol.

Families waited on Daily.
NEW MILK, BUTTER, EGGS, &c.

Local business advertisements from *Brislington Parish Magazine*, 1910.

Yew Cottage, Grove Road (now No. 5 Hollywood Road), c. 1910. Yew Cottage and Georgian Cottage, next door, date from around 1750. The centre upper window was a victim of the 1696 Window Tax which was not repealed until 1851. Emma Robinson, who could neither read nor write, seen here with her husband John, came from Ross in Wales. They opened the first newspaper shop in Brislington in 1888 in a house (now demolished) next to the smithy at the corner of what is now Hollywood Road. The family moved to Yew Cottage in 1908 where newspapers were sold from the front-room window on the left. The Robinson family remained as occupants until 1993.

Grove Road in the 1900s. This part of the present Hollywood Road was originally known as Bellevue Buildings (Nos 26–16). Eli Law is seen outside his grocers shop (now No. 16A) which he ran from approximately 1896–1932.

Bath Road, Arno's Vale, *c.* 1910. Brislington Tramway Depot in the centre was built 1898–99. The line was extended to Brislington Village in 1900, and the last tram ran into the depot in 1938. The large Victorian chapel of Arno's Court Convent on the right was demolished for road widening around 1960.

Service to celebrate the Coronation of George V on 22 June 1911. This photograph was taken from the coach house of Woodland House in Church Parade. Brislington Wesleyan Methodist Chapel (demolished 1971) is on the far left. Hayward House (also known as Brook House) in the centre background was demolished around 1926 to build public conveniences which were converted into offices for the garage on the right in 2007.

First houses in Birchwood Road, with their distinctive balustrades and roof parapets, built in the early 1900s.

First houses in Eastwood Road *c.* 1905, illustrating the architecture of the period.

Doncaster Farm, 19 October 1913. Built around 1700, this was the only owner-occupant farm in Brislington and was farmed and occupied by the Waymouth family from around 1700 until 1929. George Waymouth was the last of the family to live there. He moved to Dundry View (No. 33 Pertherton Road), Hengrove, where the family also owned property. The Hembury family were the next occupants followed by the Sutor family (approximately 1936–1941), who kept pigs and poultry. Doncaster Farm had been bought by Henry Russett, of a well-known local coach firm in the early 1930s. He offered the farmhouse and eleven acres of land, which stretched back to Victory Park, to the Sutors in 1938 for £4,500 but they could not afford to buy it. During the Second World War the farmhouse was twice badly damaged in the 1940–1941 air raids and was later used for munitions storage. It stood near the site of the Bristol Fan Co. Ltd in Broomhill Road but was demolished around 1950.

Brooklea in Wick Road, *c.* 1905. This Victorian villa was built around 1867 and was demolished around 1950. Brooklea was the home of Farnham Budgett, a well-known Bristol wholesale grocer from around 1878–1892. The last occupants were the Smith and Parry families from 1900–1943. Alderman Alfred John Smith (1843–1920) was a ship owner and director of the Newport Coal and Coke Co. of St Phillips, and was Lord Mayor of Bristol from 1905–1907. During his time as Lord Mayor, many garden parties and receptions were held in the grounds, including one for the Crimean War and Indian Mutiny Veterans Association in June 1906. Alderman Smith was a Liberal city councillor for Bedminster Ward for over twenty years and on his initiative fire-alarm boxes were set up in Bristol and the Fire Brigade was updated. He was also a leading Methodist of his day and was well known for his work with temperance societies and religious education, being superintendent of Oxford Street Methodist Chapel Sunday School in Totterdown for over thirty years. In 1899 Alderman Smith founded St Anne's Park Methodist Chapel in Langton Court Road and was its lay pastor for many years. After his death in 1920, Alderman Smith's daughter, Mrs Parry, and her family continued to live at Brooklea. His grandson, Alfred Parry (seen here as a small child, front centre), became a well-known local character who moved from Brooklea with his father, Leonard Parry, to Woodland House in Church Parade in 1943 when the house was requisitioned for American troops stationed in Brislington during the Second World War. After the war the house became derelict and was bought by Bristol City Council. The Brooklea Health Centre built nearby in 1954 perpetuates the name.

St Anne's Church, Langton Road, c. 1910. Built 1904–1909, it replaced the original 'Tin Mission Church', which had been erected on the same site in 1896. St Anne's was the first 'daughter church' of St Luke's and became a separate parish in 1909.

The Langton Court Hotel, Langton Court Road, c. 1900. Built in 1902 on the site of Langton Court, the sixteenth to seventeenth-century manor house, the oldest part of which, dating from around 1590–1610, still stands in Highworth Road. It was known locally as The Klondike, and two suggestions have been put forward for this. One is that the newly developing St Anne's area (then known as 'New Brislington') resembled the Klondike Gold Rush area of Dawson City in Yukon, USA. Another theory is that the original landlord had been at the famous 1897 gold rush and talked about nothing else!

Revd Prebendary Alfred Harman (1870–1944), Vicar of St Luke's, (1907–1918), seen with his wife, Enid, and children Margaret and Lancelot, who was born in the vicarage (Church Hill House) in 1909. Revd Harman was the last Brislington vicar to travel about the parish in a horse and carriage, the last to have a large domestic staff of nine, and the last who people remember having to curtsey to! At over 6ft tall and weighing 16st, he was an imposing figure who always wore a white bow tie and high stiff-wing collar with top hat and black frock coat.

Brislington Old Boys' Football Team, Easter Monday 1913. The team played on a pitch at Holymead Fields (now Kenneth Road area) which was a favourite venue for several local football clubs until the area was developed for house building, c. 1935.

Left: The former summer house of Wick House in Wick Road dating from the end of the eighteenth century. It still stands in the garden of No. 209 Wick Road and was being used as a bird aviary when this photograph was taken around 1912. The building was Grade II Listed in 2007.

Below: Woodbine Farm in Water Lane, *c.* 1900. The final occupants from around 1900–1938 were brothers, Ted and Tom Brean, who were farmers and coal hauliers. The farmhouse was demolished in 1938 to build houses in Gotley Road.

Right: The Black Castle, *c.* 1900s. Built in 1763–1764 by William Reeve, a copper smelter and owner of Arno's Court, as servant's quarters, stables, brew house, and laundry, in the form of a mock 'Gothic' castle, with blocks of waste slag from his copper-smelting works, which gave it its distinctive appearance. The building was later used as a farm, market garden and an antique showroom from 1911–1918 by Messrs Barbour & Little, before becoming the Bristol Tramways Co. social club in 1918. It became a public house in 1978 and was restored in 1995 and opened as a family pub and restaurant.

Below: The earliest houses in First Avenue were built around 1897 by local landowner and solicitor, James Sinnott (1845–1944), whose summer residence was Birchwood Lodge (No. 59 Birchwood Road). Mr Sinnott was instrumental in opening St Anne's Park Station in 1898, and gave St Anne's Woods as a public park in 1924. First Avenue was completed in the 1920s and 1930s when bungalows were built on the opposite side of the road.

The Three Graces (1831) by George Richmond (1809–1896), one of the most prolific portrait painters of the Victorian period and a member of the Royal Academy. The subjects are three of the daughters of Dr Edward Long Fox (1761–1835) who, in 1804, founded Brislington House Asylum on Bath Road (now Long Fox Manor). Emma Selina Fox (left) and Madelina Ker Fox (centre) did not marry, but in 1844, Anna Mary (right) married Revd George Leopold Cartwright, resident curate of Brislington 1839–1880. They lived in Brislington for the rest of their lives and are buried in St Luke's Churchyard.

2

THE ROARING TWENTIES 1919–1929

Brislington Hill, c. 1920.

The First World War brought a number of Belgian refugees to Brislington who were billeted in houses around the Kensington Hill area and at the Imperial Sports Pavilion in West Town Lane. Aeroplanes were produced at the Motor Constructional Works and the Tramway Depot on the Bath Road, and over 120 Brislington men did not return from the trenches. In 1919 Peace Day celebrations were held in the grounds of Brislington Hall (Bath Road, where the Toys R Us store is today), and in 1922 the Brislington War Memorial, paid for by public subscription, was unveiled on Kensington Hill.

Victory Park was given to the people of Brislington in 1920 as a thanksgiving for peace by Mr and Mrs Joseph Cooke-Hurle of Brislington Hill House (the current site of Gilton House flats). The following year the family moved away to Kilve Court, near Bridgwater, although most of their Brislington estate was not sold until 1946.

In 1923, the last 'Squire of Brislington', Alfred Clayfield-Ireland, died and the days of the Brislington gentry were over. The family estate was inherited by a distant cousin, Lt-Col. James St George Priaulx Armstrong, who quickly sold off most of the property and turned out many former tenants. In 1927 the Crittalls windows' factory was built on the site of the lodge of Brislington Hall, at the junction of West Town Lane and Bath Road. The Brislington Trading Estate had begun!

New roads began to be built in all directions. 1927–1928 saw the building of Brislington's first council houses in Sherwell, Bankside, Hollywood and Manworthy Roads. In 1928 the Sutton estate was built off Wick Road on the site of Broomwell House, and the in the same year the first modern houses were built in West Town Lane, transforming a tree-lined country lane of seven houses into a smart, well-to-do road of Mock Tudor suburbia. St Anne's Park council estate, which included St Anne's Park School in Lichfield Road (1929), was built between 1928 and 1931, the roads being named after English cathedrals. St Anne's Woods were opened as a public park in 1924, the gift of local landowner, James Sinnott.

The old parish of Brislington continued to be broken up. St Christopher's Church in Runswick Road was built in 1921, and was replaced by the present building ten years later, at which time the original building became the church hall. In 1926 the parishes of St Luke and St Anne were transferred from the Diocese of Bath and Wells to Bristol. St Luke's Church Hall was built in Water Lane in 1921 and became the venue for bazaars, dances and the first drama club in the area, the Brislington Players (later to become Bristol Musical Comedy Club), which was formed in 1926.

Brislington Cricket Club, formed in 1868, flourished on their ground in West Town Lane (now Kew Walk), football teams played on pitches in Holymead Fields (now Kenneth Road), and in 1925 Knowle Golf Club moved to Brislington and The Hollies in West Town Lane became their club house. The same year another of the area's big houses began a new life when Wick House was opened by the Duchess of Beaufort as a children's home run by the 'Waifs and Strays' (now the Children's Society). Formerly the home of the Hardings (of Colthurst and Harding, paint manufacturers on Bath Road), the house had been sold by the family the year before.

In 1929 a public library was opened in Hollywood Road School, and the same year saw the opening of the Ruskin Hall in Wick Road named after John Ruskin, the Victorian writer and reformer. The corrugated-iron building, erected by local Socialists from public subscription, was used for a wide variety of events over the next seventy years before being demolished in the early 2000s.

The 1920s had seen huge changes in Brislington and by the end of the decade the former Somerset village was set to be swallowed up as a new suburb of Bristol.

29th (St Anne's) Bristol Girl Guides, 1924. Back row, from left to right: Winifred Law, Nellie Thomas, Alice Brindle. Front row: Kathleen Gilliam, Kathleen Dewey, ?Law. Formed in 1924 the company was amalgamated into a district unit (22nd Bristol) in 1993.

Brislington Fire Brigade, c. 1920. Formed by Brislington Parish Council in 1902, this brigade photograph was taken in the fire station in Hollywood Road which they used from 1912–1933. The building was recently converted into a private house. From left to right: Bert Watts, Ron Anderson, Alfie Knight, Hector Smart.

Left: West's undertaker's yard, Bath Road, Brislington Village, 1920s (now the site of Brislington Motor Services Ltd). Frederick John West (1867–1926) is seen left of the ladder. The West family came to Brislington in 1861 and ran their undertaking and monumental mason's business from the 1890s to the 1950s and also ran the village post office at Albert House in Brislington Square for three generations from the end of the nineteenth century until 1955.

Below: West's undertaker's yard, Bath Road, Brislington Village, 1920s. Brislington Hill is off to the left. Part of the site was let to Williams & Stone, builders and decorators (note the sign on wall) from around 1920–1972.

St Anne's Park Station in the 1920s. Opened on 23 May 1898 on the Bristol-Bath GWR line which had originally opened fifty years earlier in 1840, the station closed on 5 January 1970.

St Anne's Church fancy-dress football match, 21 May 1921, believed to have been played in the grounds of Brooklea in Wick Road. The game was a fund-raising event for the church hall which was built in Salisbury Road in 1921. A scout hut was added in 1946 and the buildings were demolished in 1989 when the land was sold to pay for the reordering of St Anne's Church. Candy Court flats now stand on the site. Revd H.S. Urch (Vicar, 1919–1924) is seen as a barrister on the left.

R. E. Ware,
395 BATH ROAD, BRISLINGTON
Near Tramways Depot.

District Agent for B.S.A. and the ALL-STEEL, RALEIGH BICYCLES.

Repairs Prompt and Reliable.

Established 1881.

R. W. CHOWN,
Builder and House Decorator,
Sanitary and Ventilating Engineer,
FREELAND HOUSE, BRISLINGTON.

Range Boilers Cleaned, Etc.

H. REX,
(Late T. BAKER & SON)
Dairyman and Pork Butcher,
10 Sandy Park Rd., Brislington
Families in all parts of District waited upon daily with Pure New Milk, Butter Eggs and Cream.
Noted for Dairy-Fed Pork and Home-cured Bacon.
Always a good Supply of Cooked Meats

F. J. HEDGELAND,
Painter, Paperhanger, Grainer, etc.
26 WICK ROAD., BRISLINGTON.
BRISTOL.

GENERAL HOUSE REPAIRS.
Prompt personal attention given to all Orders.

Try GOULD'S
HIGH-CLASS BREAD AND CONFECTIONERY
Agent for the "Allinson" Wholemeal Bread.
MACHINE BAKERIES,
Lincoln Street, Barton Hill, Bristol

A. M. PROSSER,
SANDY PARK ROAD,
Plumber, Gasfitter and Decorator.

ELECTRIC BELLS FITTED.
Repairs of all kinds promptly attended to.

H. W. L. FOOT, Butcher,
Winchester and Bath Roads,
BRISLINGTON.

Cooked Meats, Sausages and Pickled Tongues Always in Stock.
Tel. 79.   DELIVERIES to all parts DAILY

MORRIS

Hampstead
(RICHARD F. LEAT)
Tel. 7366. **Garage,**
AUTOMOBILE GENERAL ENGINEERS.

Overhauls.   Accessories.
Accumulators Charged.

King Road,
BRISLINGTON.

Local business advertisements from *Brislington Parish Magazine*, 1929.

Right: Bert Stowell (1879–1929) in the vegetable garden at The Chestnuts (now off Bonville Road), where he worked as a stable boy and later as a gardener for the Vowles and Williams families from 1894 until his death.

Below: The wedding of Mabel Maud Stowell and Robert Smith in October 1921 outside Oakenhill Cottages, which still stand off Bonville Road. The Stowell family lived at No. 2 from the 1880s to the 1940s.

Left: Georgiana Cavendish, Duchess of Devonshire (1757–1806), painted by Thomas Gainsborough in 1786. The scandalous celebrated beauty, socialite and political campaigner is believed to have skated on the pond in the grounds of West Town House (now No. 11 West Town Park), possibly on her visit to Bath in 1782.

Below: The eighteenth-century pond in the grounds of West Town House in the 1920s. The man-made pond was drained and filled with rubble in 1962 to build houses in West Town Grove.

Right: Holly Cottages in School Road, 1920s. The cottages (now Nos 102 and 100A School Road, located at the junction with Clayfield Road) are believed to date from around 1740. William Pollard was gardener at Brislington Hall and his family occupied the right-hand cottage, *c.* 1917–1925. The cottages were probably the village 'Dame School' before becoming the infant school of St Luke's Church School in 1822. The cottages became two dwellings after 1859 when the new church school was built, and were later owned by Bugler's Coaches who set up their business at No. 102 School Road around 1948. The family owned both cottages until 1986, and ran their bus and coach business from the premises behind until very recently.

Below: Homeside, Brislington Hill in the 1920s. The Skilling family, seen here outside this Georgian house, were occupants 1907–1928. Alfred Skilling was the clerk to Brislington Parish Council for many years. The house stood at the bottom of Brislington Hill and was demolished for the present shops in 1969.

Left: Dr Arthur Wellesley McClelland on the right practiced as a GP at No. 655 Bath Road from around 1905–1946. His stepson, Leslie Darby, is on the left, and Dr McClelland's chauffeur, Arthur Sobey, is centre.

Below: Langton Court Road, St Anne's, *c.* 1926–1928.

Top of Bristol Hill, early 1920s. The entrance to Talbot Lane and the wall of Hemplow House (demolished for Beeches Grove and Hawburn Close in 1969) are off left. Eagle House was demolished in 1934 to build Eagle Road off left of the picture. Brislington Congregational Church (now United Reformed church) and The Grove are centre.

Hopkins shop, No. 12 Sandy Park Road, 1925. The Misses Clara and Martha Hopkins ran the tobacconist and sweet shop from approximately 1922–1950, following on from their father, John Hopkins, who took over the shop around 1917. Their niece, Elsie Payne from Glasgow (seen on left of doorway) went on to have a career as a Radio Scotland presenter on *Children's Hour* and *The McFlannels* in the 1940s. The shop sold loose tobacco and snuff, weighed out on minute scales, and marzipan Easter eggs. Sweets were then about 2d a quarter (about 1p in today's money).

A charabanc outing from Brislington Wesleyan Methodist Chapel preparing to leave Brislington Square, early 1920s. Forsey's butcher's shop on the far left (now an Indian takeaway) was the village butcher's shop from around 1800–1979. In about 1904 Walter Forsey acquired the shop, and his family continued to run it for three generations until its final closure in 1979. Mr Forsey came from Norton Fitzwarren and began with a butcher's stall at Taunton Market. He came to Bristol in 1892 and opened a butcher's shop at No. 117 Oxford Street, Totterdown, before taking over the shop in Brislington Square. The family operated both shops until about 1930. After Walter's death in 1920, the business continued to be run by his widow Polly and son Frank, who was described as 'a typical old village butcher, a portly gentleman in his traditional blue and white striped apron, who was jovial and well liked'. Frank and his son Peter went into partnership in 1957 and the following year opened a greengrocer's shop next door. After Frank retired in 1964, Peter took over the business completely and remained until it closed in 1979.

Next to the shop, Forsey's had one of the last registered slaughter houses (seen on the far right), but this closed in 1939 when all animal slaughtering was centralised in Bristol. Animals were grazed in fields off School Road rented from the Cooke-Hurle estate (now covered by Jean Road). Mondays and Wednesdays were traditional 'killing days', which began at 4 a.m. as it took several hours to boil up the tripe and make dripping and so on. The family also made all their own sausages and seasonings on the premises. In the days before fridges and freezers people used to shop two or three times a day for each meal – bacon for breakfast, sausages for supper etc. A piece of steak cost half-a-crown (12½p). All orders were delivered by bicycle and at one time four errand boys were employed.

3
BRISLINGTON INTO BRISTOL 1930–1939

Sandy Park Road, c. 1935.

In 1933 Brislington finally became fully included within the boundary of the City and County of Bristol and Brislington Parish Council, which had run the village since 1894, was abolished.

From 1935–1938 Holymead Fields, where medieval pilgrims had gathered on the last stage of their journey to St Anne's Chapel and the Holy Well, were built on, becoming the residential streets of Kenneth, Warrington, Hulse, and Callington Roads. The Broomhill area, traditionally a well-known spot for local courting couples, with its large fields and farmland, began to be built up with bungalows appearing along Broomhill Road. The new neighbourhood was served with shops along Broomhill Road and a pub, the Good Intent, which opened in 1939.

Eagle House was demolished in 1934 to build Eagle Road, and from 1936 houses were built in the grounds of West Town House to become the West Town Park area. Manor Farm, Brislington's medieval manor house, the oldest part of which is believed to have dated back to Saxon times, was sadly demolished in 1933 for the Imperial Sports Ground in West Town Lane. At the other end of the road, at the Brislington Hill junction, a small rank of shops and a police station were built in 1936.

During the thirties more factories began to appear along the Bath Road, including the Trist-Draper 'Top Dog' works (1930), Leyland Motors (1931), Smiths Crisps (1936) and Coca-Cola (1939). The CWS clothing factory was built on Kensington Hill in 1936 following the demolition of Kensington Place, which had been taken over by the factory in 1920. A Co-op laundry and a dairy were also opened in Whitby Road in 1938. As other CWS factories were established, the road was once dubbed 'Co-op Alley' containing, in addition to the laundry and dairy, a butter factory, soft-drinks plant and a boot-repair factory.

Despite the growing urbanisation, farming and market gardening continued to operate with around twelve dairymen still in business. Gradually, however, the number of working farms declined and several were demolished for more housing development, including Linton Farm which became Runnymead Avenue (1936), St Anne's Farm for the Wootton Road area (1937), and Woodbine Farm for Gotley Road (1938).

Recreational needs were also catered for. In 1931 Brislington Hall on the Bath Road was opened as the Lido Spa hotel and nightclub, but the venture was short lived and the hall was demolished two years later. In the same year the first talking pictures were shown at the Brislington Cinema in Sandy Park Road. The cinema was owned and run by the Tomkins family for nearly forty years and was altered and enlarged in 1937 to compete with the new Ritz Cinema built at the corner of Bristol Hill and Warrington Road. Care had to be taken while the Ritz was under construction to avoid damage to a large oak tree near the site, which had been planted in 1863 to commemorate the wedding of the Prince and Princess of Wales (later Edward VII and Queen Alexandra). The cinema has been partially demolished and replaced by a shop, but the tree still lives on! The Ritz was officially opened in October 1938 by British film comedian, Wally Patch. Hailed as the 'Showpiece of the West', it was designated for conversion to a hospital at the time of the Munich Crisis in September 1938.

In 1937 the country celebrated the Coronation of George VI, street parties were held and there was a large fête in the grounds of The Beeches, which was part of the Brislington House asylum estate. Dr Francis Elliot Fox distributed Coronation mugs to local children. Only two years later, however, the brief peace of twenty-one years was shattered and Brislington found itself at war again.

Delivery vans outside Robertson's 'Golden Shred Works' in Water Lane in the 1930s. When it was built in 1914 the factory was in a completely rural setting and by the 1950s had become the biggest jam factory in Europe.

The famous 'Golden Shred' marmalade being loaded outside Robertson's Jam Factory in the 1930s. As the public taste for jam declined in post-war years, the factory closed in 1980 and was demolished for the Tesco store which opened in 1985.

Women working at Terrell's Rope Works at Arno's Vale in the 1930s. Brislington's first industrial factory, Terrell's was established at Welsh Back in Bristol in the 1870s and moved to Canon's Marsh in the 1880s, before moving to Brislington in 1902. They made all sizes of rope up to 4in hawsers and also held the contract for braided piston packing for locomotives on the Great Western Railway.

Rope being made at Terrell's Rope Works in the 1930s. The firm was taken over by British Ropes in 1964 and closed the following year. The factory was demolished and the Burger King restaurant now stands on the site.

The Joseph Lucas Ltd motor accessories building on Bath Road at Arno's Vale, c. 1933. This stood next to what is now the Majestic wine warehouse. Opened in 1928, Lucas was part of a national company supplying electrical components for the motor industry. The Brislington branch was a distribution depot for Lucas and associated products. It closed in 1978 and was demolished. The site has remained empty ever since.

Logo of 'Top Dog', the Trist-Draper brake and clutch-lining works on Bath Road which opened in 1930. The building was designed by Albert Thomas, a partner of architect Sir Edwin Luytens. It closed in 1985 and was demolished. The Toys R Us store now stands on the site.

Painting by A. Watkins of the opening night of the Ritz Cinema at the junction of Bristol Hill and Warrington Road. The Ritz, hailed as 'The Showpiece of the West' and 'Bristol's New Luxury Cinema', was designed by well-known Bristol cinema architect W.H. Watkins and was officially opened on 8 October 1938 by British film comedian Wally Patch (1888–1970). The distinctive cream, stucco Art Deco building with green-glazed roof seated 1,400 people and the glamorous opening night was attended by both locals and well-to-do guests in evening dress. They included the Lord Mayor of Bristol, Alderman J.J. Milton, and Chairman of Directors George Allen, who owned several other Bristol cinemas. The first film shown was *A Yank at Oxford*, starring heart-throb of the day Robert Taylor and rising British star Vivien Leigh.

This painting was presented to the cinema by W.H. Watkins and hung in the foyer for thirty years. Jack Day, the last manager of the Ritz, presented it to Fred Kilburn, the last projectionist who screened the final film, the X-rated *Valley of the Dolls* starring Susan Hayward and Sharon Tate, on the closing night, 20 July 1968.

After lying empty for two years the Ritz was partially demolished and opened as a Budgens supermarket. It later became a carpet showroom, a freezer centre, a Kwik Save supermarket and is now a DIY store.

The Ritz withstood wartime bombing and the rise of television in the post-war years and had a brief life of only thirty years but is still fondly remembered today. Around fifty former patrons and staff gave their memories as research for a musical play, *Remember The Ritz?*, written by Jonathan Rowe to celebrate the twentieth anniversary in 2008 of St Luke's Church Players and seventy and forty years since the opening and closing of the Ritz. The highly acclaimed production was performed in St Luke's Church Hall in May 2008.

Horace Davids, the first manger of the Ritz (1938–1940), taken from outside the Ritz, c. 1939. Bristol Hill is on the right. Warrington House, on the left, has been a dental practice ever since it was built in the late 1930s. Horace Davids lived in West Town Lane and had previously been manager of the Regent Cinema in Castle Street, Bristol, for seven years. He is said to have left the Ritz with a week's takings and the lady cashier! Edward Heybyrne, who took over as manager, stayed at the Ritz for eighteen years and lived in Runswick Road where his family still live today. A very popular and well-respected man, he always wore a bowler hat and dinner suit when on duty.

After he left, the Ritz began to decline during the 'Teddy Boy' era of the 1950s. Short-term managers followed and the ownership changed several times. Fred Seymour was manager from around 1960–1964, followed by Jack Day, who was to become the last manager during 1964–1968. Jack Day was a well-known character in the business and was also manager of the Charlton cinema in Keynsham for twenty-three years. In 1964 he introduced pop-concert nights featuring local amateur pop groups, including 'Pete Budd and The Rebels'. Pete Budd grew up in Brislington in Repton Road and then Pendennis Park, and later found fame as one of 'The Wurzels'.

The Ritz had its fair share of celebrity customers, including popular 1950s pianist Winifred Attwell, singing stars and 1959 British Eurovision Song Contest contenders Pearl Carr and Teddy Johnson, actors Richard Pasco and Tony Britton (father of Fern Britton from ITV's *This Morning*), film comedian Norman Wisdom and entertainer Bruce Forsyth. The site is said to be haunted by the ghost of a customer of the Ritz who died on the premises, in the toilets. Over many years people have heard ghostly footsteps late at night and experienced other unexplained supernatural events.

Mrs Yda Richardson (a member of Wills tobacco manufacturing family) laying the foundation stone of St Cuthbert's Church, Sandy Park Road, 28 February 1932. The church was consecrated on 11 February 1933 by the Bishop of Bristol, Rt Revd George Nickson. The building replaced the tin Mission Church which was erected in January 1906 and stood at the top of what is now Allison Road.

St Anne's Park Methodist Church, Langton Court Road, in the 1930s. This 1936 extension was added to the original building which opened in 1899. The church was closed in 1978 and demolished for St Anne's Court flats in 1982.

Right: Coronation House, No. 46 Brislington Hill. This distinctive Art Deco house was built in 1937 by H.F.N. Greenhill & Sons from a design shown at the Bristol Ideal Home exhibition that year, which 70,000 people queued to see. This daily landmark to thousands of commuters driving through Brislington was used as a location in the 1979 film *Radio On*, which featured singer Sting and actress Sandy Ratcliff, who was later 'Sue Osman' in *EastEnders*.

Below: No.126 Broomhill Road, 1935. This new bungalow was the first home of Clifford and Edna Long until 1960, and was surrounded by fields and farmland when it was built in 1935. Mr Long was employed at Crittalls Windows on Bath Road and walked across the fields to work.

Harry Carey (1877–1940), dairyman with cows in fields off School Road in 1930. In the first decades of the twentieth century there were sixteen working farms in Brislington, many of them dairy, and also about a dozen dairy rounds. Milk, which cost 2½d pint (about 1p in today's money), was ladled out to customers from churns until bottles were introduced in the 1940s. Harry Carey ran a dairy from No. 3 The Square in Brislington village from the early 1920s, which was continued by his son, Gordon (1915–1996) until about 1948.

The family, who still live in Brislington today, came to the village in the 1870s from Christon, near Banwell in Somerset. Charles Carey (1847–1906) ran a butcher's shop at No. 1 Bellevue Road (now Bellevue Park) from about 1880 until his death. In 1914 his son, Harry, married Alice Watts, who had been a parlour maid for Revd Alfred Harman at St Luke's Vicarage (Church Hill House). The family rented the three-acre 'Glebe Land' fields, seen here, from St Luke's Church for fifty years until 1937 when the land was sold for housing development. The site is now covered by the area around Castlegate House and Granston Close near Brislington Cemetery, which was opened in 1905. The Carey family also rented Oakenhill Farm around 1928–1950 and an orchard at Brislington Hall. Harry Carey died in 1940 after being run over by a bread van while delivering milk in Hollywood Road. He foresaw the outbreak of the Second World War when several white bull calves were born, which were traditionally seen as a bad omen and portent of evil.

A view of the kitchen garden in Church Hill belonging to Woodland House (out of picture). The picture is taken in about 1930 from the Engine House in Hollywood Road. The Engine House was referred to by George Weare Braikenridge of Broomwell House in the 1820s as The Old Fire Engine House. It is believed to date from the 1790s and is said to have been connected in some way with the collieries which once operated in Brislington, although this seems unlikely.

This photograph was taken by a member of the Poole family who lived at The Engine House from around 1923–1963. E.A.W. Poole & Sons were local builders and the name is perpetuated in the Old Poole's Yard development, built in 2004 on the site of their former works yard. Water Cottages on the left were probably demolished in 1965 for No. 9 Church Hill. Freeland House and Freeland Cottage opposite were bombed in 1940 and later demolished, the site remaining empty until Nos 14 and 16 Church Hill were built about 1977. Freeland House is said to have been the site of the pilgrim's hostelry where Henry VII rested on his pilgrimage to St Anne's Chapel in 1486 and was a 'school for young ladies' in the 1850s and 1860s. Robert Chown, builder, decorator and painter, was the last occupant from around 1885.

The bridge, greenhouse and garage were swept away in the 'Great Flood' of 1968. St Luke's Church School can be seen in the far centre distance. It was opened in 1859, replacing the original church school located on three sites which began in 1822, and was the 'village school' for eighty-three years until it was bombed in an air raid in 1942. The buildings were demolished in 1953 and the schoolmaster's house is all that survives today in Rock Close. St Luke's Church can be seen at the top right.

The pressing room of the CWS Clothing Factory on Kensington Hill, Bath Road, in the early 1930s. Ern Dodge, on the far left, was the foreman. The factory originally opened in 1920 in part of Kensington Place, a terrace of three houses built around 1795. By the 1890s these had all been taken for business use and were demolished in 1936 to erect a purpose-built clothing factory which closed in 1980. Later taken over by office furniture business, John Peer Ltd, it has been derelict for many years.

St Luke's Church Tennis Club around 1933 at the church sports ground off Broomhill Road, near Doncaster Farm. Phillip Eden, seen in the centre as a boy, later ran Sandy Park Post Office for over thirty years from approximately 1955.

St Anne's Park Girls School in the mid-1930s. The school in Lichfield Road, St Anne's Park, opened in 1929 and is now a junior school.

Wick Road School class in the 1930s. Opened in 1905, the school is now Holymead Juniors.

Alderman William Winchester and Mrs Florence Winchester, Lord Mayor and Lady Mayoress of Bristol 1938–1939. Alderman Winchester was a Labour Bristol City councillor for twenty-two years, representing St George Ward from 1919 until becoming an alderman in 1932. A sometime governor of Colston Boys' School and chairman of Bristol East Labour Party, he was formerly a photographer with a business which he ran from his home at No. 4 Langton Road, St Anne's.

The last tram to run from Brislington village to Brislington Tram Depot on Bath Road, 2 September 1938. The building is now occupied by Bristol City Council Contract Services.

4

WAR AND AUSTERITY
1940–1949

Air raid damage, Grove Park Road, 1940.

The outbreak of the Second World War had made an immediate impact on Brislington when the 'Bristol's Own' 50th tank regiment was stationed at various venues, including Woodland House in Church Parade, Kensington House on Bath Road (now the site of the PDSA), and The Beeches in Broomhill Road. The Beeches later became the base for a Royal Engineers bomb disposal unit.

A 'Happy Warrior' canteen was set up for the troops in St Luke's Church Hall in Water Lane and was later transferred to the old Congregational chapel in Kenneth Road. The church hall became a 'Garrison Theatre' for the tank corps, who enjoyed monthly Friday-night shows featuring radio and stage stars of the day, such as Randolph Sutton, Elsie and Doris Waters, Jack Warner and Anne Shelton. After the tank regiment left, St Luke's Church Hall was requisitioned as a mortuary for air-raid victims.

Hemplow House in Talbot Road was commandeered as a civil-defence centre and was used by the auxiliary fire service. The Grove Hall on Wick Road became an air-raid shelter and then a rest centre for bombed-out families, and was visited by Queen Mary in December 1940. She made several more visits to Brislington including Wick Road School, Robertson's Jam Factory and the 'Top Dog' works on Bath Road. George VI also made a private visit to Brislington House Asylum in 1940 where several bombs had fallen in the grounds.

In June 1940 some of the first bombs dropped over Bristol fell in Brislington, with damage and loss of life in Glenarm Walk, Pendennis Park and Grove Park Road. Several historic buildings were badly damaged during the Blitz and were later demolished, including Brislington Hill House, St Luke's Church School and Heath House in the grounds of Brislington House Asylum.

Brislington was never to suffer a Nazi invasion but the area was invaded and occupied by a friendlier and more welcome force – the United States Army – who were stationed in the area in 1943 as they prepared for the D-Day invasion in June 1944. American troops were billeted in private homes all over Brislington and a large camp was set up in fields off School Road, now covered by Clayfield Road. Brooklea, a large Victorian villa in Wick Road, was requisitioned for their use and the Co-op Bakery in Whitby Road became their headquarters where, it was said, 20 million francs were stored, along with a vast store of maps and equipment ready for the Normandy invasion. The GIs invited local residents to dances at the School Road camp, a 'Jitterbug Marathon' dance was held at the Ruskin Hall, and on one occasion the Ritz cinema was taken over for a big-band concert.

On 8 May 1945 St Luke's Church bells rang out for peace and VE (Victory in Europe) Day was celebrated with street parties all over Brislington, followed a few months later by VJ (Victory in Japan) Day. As the country moved into the post-war era, prefabricated bungalows – 'prefabs' – for home-coming troops were built in Broomhill and West Town Lane. The last of these were demolished in the early years of the twenty-first century.

In 1948 John Wright & Sons, printers, became the first post-war factory to open on the officially designated Brislington Trading Estate.

Mr and Mrs Robert Cuff in the garden of Hillside House, West Town Lane, *c.* 1940 The family lived at the house, about which very little is known, from 1933–1958. Between 1925–1939 Mr Cuff built many houses in Brislington, including Hardenhuish Road, Savoy Road, Bloomfield Road, Martingale Road, Harrow Road and Cuffington Avenue, which is named after him.

Mrs Marcia Cuff (daughter-in-law of Mrs and Mrs Cuff) on the front steps of Hillside House, *c.* 1940. The house was surrounded by grounds and was enclosed on three sides by high walls and an iron entrance gate. The imposing entrance had marble steps and granite pillars. The house was demolished around 1959–60 to build Callington Road flats.

George's Sports Ground, off West Town Lane, c. 1940. The ground was ploughed up to 'Dig for Victory' in the Second World War. These three acres provided 8 tons per acre yield of potatoes. The Grace Park estate was built on the site in the 1980s, all roads being named after famous British cricketers, Hammond Place, Grace Park Road and so on. Hungerford Road is now behind the trees on the right.

Father Christmas arrives in Hampstead Road in an AFS fire engine during the Second World War. The Auxiliary Fire Service was based in Hemplow House, at the bottom of Talbot Road which was commandeered as a civil defence centre.

Brislington Scouts parade along Bristol Hill in 1944, past the Ritz Cinema and the bungalow, Raparee (No. 20 Bristol Hill), built c. 1925.

Dr Francis Elliot Fox and Mrs Ethel Fox of Brislington House Asylum on Bath Road (now Long Fox Manor) and their baby son, Francis David Bonville Fox, known as 'Bonnie', at his christening on 15 June 1944. Dr Fox died in 1947, and was the last 'Dr Fox' of Brislington, the family having run the private mental asylum for over 140 years. Mrs Ethel Fox was a former matron of the asylum and ran it until it closed in 1952. She continued to occupy Swiss Cottage, in the grounds, until her death in 1989 and was the last member of the family to live in Brislington.

VE Day (Victory in Europe) street party in Churchill Road, 8 May 1945.

VE Day street party in Allison Avenue, 8 May 1945.

Cherry Orchard Farm, 1946. This seventeenth/eighteenth-century farmhouse, formerly part of the Cooke-Hurle estate, stood at what is now the junction of Stockwood Lane and Hungerford Road. It was sold at auction in 1946 with all the remaining Cooke-Hurle property in Brislington. The Taylor family were the last occupants of Cherry Orchard Farm from the early 1930s until it was demolished in the mid-1950s to build the Hungerford Road estate.

Scotland Bottom Farm (or Lower Scotland Farm), Stockwood Lane, 1946. This property was also part of the Cooke-Hurle estate. The last occupant from around 1938 was Roland Young. The building was demolished around 1956/1957 for the Stockwood tip, which itself closed in 1989.

A. GREENSLADE
(Proprietress: A. G. Summerfield)

Specialist in High-Class Footwear Repairs

Hand-sewn Work Done
Best Materials only used

THE SQUARE, Brislington

PUREST DRUGS — PROMPT ATTENTION — TOILET GOODS — TELEPHONE 76986

W. L. J. BARWICK, M.P.S.
8 WEST TOWN LANE, BRISLINGTON

National Health Prescriptions carefully dispensed — Invalid and Baby Requisites
Photographic Supplies — Films developed

D. G. THORN Purveyor & Bacon Curer

Telephone 76249   **14 West Town Lane, Brislington**

W. J. Jarrett
Florist, Fruiterer & Greengrocer
Weddings, Wreaths and Altar Flowers a Speciality

Telephone 76279   **367 BATH ROAD, BRISTOL 4**

MODERATE CHARGES — TELEPHONE 41639 — ESTIMATES FREE

Modern Decorating Specialists — **LEIGH BROS.** — Property Maintenance Contractors

35 KENNETH ROAD, BRISLINGTON 4 — **42 VALENTINE CLOSE**, KNOWLE 4

Flowers, Fruit & Vegetables — Telephone 78500 — Fresh supplies of Fish daily

R. T. FISHER
10 WEST TOWN LANE, Brislington

LOWELL BALDWIN LTD.
WHOLESALE & RETAIL COAL & COKE MERCHANTS

Phone 25041 (6 lines)   Telegrams: "Cobbles, Bristol"
Depots—AVON STREET WHARF   REDCLIFF WHARF
WAPPING WHARF   SHIREHAMPTON STATION

6/8 Redcliffe Hill

FRESH FISH DAILY — **L. LINE & SON** — GAME AND POULTRY

at

20 KENSINGTON PARK ROAD, BRISLINGTON

Local business advertisements from *Brislington Parish Magazine*, 1948.

Wedding of Marjorie Harris and Alexander (Alec) Fyfe, 1 June 1946. The bridesmaids were her sisters Elizabeth (Betty) and Esme, and her sister-in-law Phyllis Harris. The wedding photos were taken outside her home at No. 7 Sunnydene on the Sutton Estate, because there were so many weddings when the troops came home at the end of the war, that they could not get a photographer at the relevant time at St Anne's Church, where they were married. Betty was married only a few months later, and due to rationing, the bridesmaids' dresses, in pale blue, were recycled.

Marjorie, with her parents (Edgar and Lilian), her brother, two sisters, and their mother's younger brother, were one of the first families to move on to the Sutton Estate, in the 1920s. The register at Wick Road Infants' School shows all three sisters enrolling there, but their elder brother, Ron, was already at school at Redcliffe, which he continued to attend, walking there and back every day!

The Sutton Estate was one of several built around the country by the Sutton Dwellings Trust 'for occupation by the poor of London and other towns and populous places in England' (William Sutton Homes Website). Completed in 1928, it was the first estate in the south-west of England. Although the houses had bathrooms, the toilet was located outside the back door next to the coal house, and the living-room fireplaces incorporated a bread oven! The gardens were very large, enabling green-fingered residents to grow enough vegetables to feed entire families, or even keep chickens. The houses were upgraded over the years, bringing toilets indoors, and installing central heating and new kitchens. From 1992 to 2005 the estate underwent a major phased redevelopment. The rather narrow streets have been retained, but the houses now have off-road parking, facilitated by setting the houses further back and reducing the size of the back gardens.

Programme covers for Bristol International and Modern Home Exhibition September-October 1948 (*left*) and the Bristol Ideal Home, Industrial and Fashion Exhibition 1949 (*right*).

The 1948 was held in fields off Bath Road on Brislington Trading Estate. The programme stated: 'The City Corporation have obtained ... approximately forty-six acres of land ... for the purpose of extending the industrial development of this locality. The estate will be developed to ensure architectural and utilitarian harmony'.

The 1949 exhibition, also held on the Brislington Trading Estate, included a variety theatre where visitors could witness a range of entertainments such as 'Rayanne – the World's Wonder Girl – who mystified Stewart Granger'; Musaire-Music Melody Maker; a fashion parade by 'London's Leading Mannequins'; and a exhibition bout by boxer Freddie Mills, the then light heavyweight champion of the world.

St Cuthbert's Players' production of *For Goodness Sake*, February 1948, in the Crypt Room of St Cuthbert's Church, Sandy Park Road. Having formed the group only the previous year, this three act comedy play directed by Betty Hawkins and John Pilgrim was their first full-length production. For over twenty-one years the group put on forty-three plays and over seventy members trod the boards coming from not only Brislington but also Stockwood, Bishop Sutton, Kingswood, Pensford and Longwell Green.

The group was forced to close in 1968 after a Theatres Act required fireproofing, lighting and fire exits which could not be fulfilled in the crypt room. Many familiar names entertained audiences between 1947–1968 including Juliet Hollyman, Gertrude West, Carol Tiley (now Compton), Bob Thomas, Vivien Parsons, Harold Miller, John Leece, June Maynard (later McCarthy), June Rockett, Ken Spear, Lynda Harris, Maureen Forsey, Ivy Dredge, Doreen Scott (now Mallard), Lloyd Virtue, Evelyn Hedges, Mildred Frayne, Mary Woodman (later Wintle), Julian Todd, Edwin Clark, and particularly Roger Vaughan, Dinah Silcox (now Moon), Maidie Kembery and Sid Spiers, who between them made seventy-two appearances and also produced eighteen of the full-length productions. Sid Spiers was also treasurer for the whole twenty-one years, and later took over the chairmanship from founder chairman Ken Spear.

VE Day party, 8 May 1945, for residents in Sandwich Road, held in the St Anne's Park Brotherhood and Sisterhood building in Wick Road.

Gordon Carey (1915–1996) working at Oakenhill Farm, off Bonville Road, in the late 1940s. The Carey family were the last to farm at Oakenhill.

5

YOU'VE NEVER HAD IT SO GOOD 1950–1959

St Luke's Church youth club, 1953.

St Luke's Church tower was floodlit to celebrate the Festival of Britain in 1951 as the post-war years of austerity and rationing gave way to the more affluent fifties and the 'You've never had it so good' Conservative government of Harold MacMillan. The 1953 Coronation was heralded as the dawn of a new 'Elizabethan Age' and the country celebrated the crowning of Queen Elizabeth II. Many people watched the event on new television sets bought especially for the occasion. In Brislington there were the usual street parties. Special events were held in many venues including the Ruskin Hall, Hollywood Road and Wick Road Schools and local scouts organised a large 'Coronation barbeque' in a field near The Chestnuts off Bonville Road.

Although the frantic house building of earlier decades was now over, new dwellings were still needed to rehouse people from condemned inner-city property such as St Philip's Marsh, as well as to relocate some prefab residents. The Hungerford Road estate was built during 1953–1957 on 824 acres of agricultural land and included Brislington Comprehensive School, which opened in 1956. Two other infant and junior schools were also built in the decade – Broomhill (1951 and 1956) and West Town Lane (1954 and 1958).

The growing popularity of television and more up-to-date cinemas signalled the closure of the Brislington Cinema in Sandy Park Road in 1956 after forty-three years of service to the local community. The following year saw the founding of a new Brislington football club. Matches were played initially in Arno's Park, moving to Victory Park in 1960 and finally their present home in Ironmould Lane in 1978.

Corner shops continued to thrive, with some grocery and other deliveries by horse and cart still taking place around Brislington, but in 1958 the area's first purpose-built supermarket was opened by the Co-op in Broomhill Road. The village blacksmith had already given way to a garage in the mid-1940s and in 1959 Arthur Heal left Eastwood Farm, Broomhill, one of the last working farms in Brislington. Mr Heal continued his milk round until 1981 and was Brislington's last surviving dairyman. Its rural atmosphere was fast disappearing.

Brislington Trading Estate grew rapidly in the 1950s and 1960s with the development of industry on both sides of the Bath Road to the east of the village. New factories included Modern Engineering, Godwin Warren Electrical Engineers, Lyons Bakery, Schweppes, Gallahers tobacco manufacturers, Oxo and Channel Plastics.

Brislington also has its own permanent reminder of the days of the Cold War of the 1950s, in the shape of the Bristol War Room on the Government Buildings site in Flowers Hill. Built in 1954 as an atomic bomb-proof bunker, the whole of the South West would have been ruled from Brislington in the event of an atomic war with communist Russia.

The fifteenth-century tower of St Luke's Church, floodlit for the Festival of Britain, 1951.

St Cuthbert's Players on a Whit Monday outing, 5 June 1950. Members include: Jim Kembery, Peter Evans, Jose Hanney, Sid Spiers, Ray Thompson, Viv Parsons, Dinah Silcox, June Maynard, Ruth and Roger Vaughan.

Brislington Drama Club production of *Bonaventure*, April 1952, at St Luke's Church Hall in Water Lane. The club was formed in 1948 by curate, Revd Denys Evans, and performed farces, comedies and dramas over more than thirty years, moving to the present church hall in Church Parade in 1964. Brislington Drama Club was dissolved in about 1980, but was succeeded by the present group, St Luke's Church Players, formed in 1988 by the Vicar Revd Peter Dyson.

Broomhill Road, summer 1957. Brislington and St Anne's District Scouts celebrate fifty years of scouting with a procession to Wick House. The building on the left is the original prefabricated 'Robin' hangar Co-op store built in 1947. This was replaced by the present building, Brislington's first supermarket, which opened on the same site in December 1958. The architect was Sam Wyatt, later a well-known local councillor, who lived in Eastwood Road.

This picture shows the scouts having arrived in the grounds of Wick House in Wick Road. Built around 1790, Wick House became a children's home run by the 'Waifs and Strays' (now The Children's Society) in 1925. It closed in 1981 when it became a nursing home and has been a refugee hostel since 2003.

A. GREENSLADE (Proprietress: A. G. Sommerfield)
Specialist in High-Class Footwear Repairs
Hand-sewn Work Done
Best Materials only used
THE SQUARE, Brislington

PUREST DRUGS PROMPT ATTENTION TOILET GOODS TELEPHONE 76986

W. L. J BARWICK, M.P.S.
8 WEST TOWN LANE, BRISLINGTON

National Health Prescriptions carefully dispensed
Photographic Supplies
Invalid and Baby Requisites
Films developed

D. G. THORN Purveyor & Bacon Curer

Telephone 76249   **14 West Town Lane, Brislington**

"JUDITH ALLEN"
LADIES AND CHILDREN'S HIGH-CLASS HAIRDRESSER
Machine and Machineless Permanent Waving   Tinting and Bleaching
16a HOLLYWOOD ROAD, BRISLINGTON

THE BLACK CAT
(Agent for Cadena Ltd.)

CAKES, PASTRIES, SWEETS, CHOCOLATES, ICE CREAM, CIGARETTES
WEDDING AND BIRTHDAY CAKES A SPECIALITY

50 BRISTOL HILL   Telephone 77540

Flowers, Fruit & Vegetables   Telephone 78500   Fresh Supplies of Fish Daily

R. T. FISHER
10 WEST TOWN LANE, Brislington

LOWELL BALDWIN LTD.   WHOLESALE & RETAIL COAL & COKE MERCHANTS

Phone 25041 (6 lines)   Telegrams: "Cobbles, Bristol."
Depots—AVON STREET WHARF   REDCLIFFE WHARF
WAPPING WHARF   SHIREHAMPTON STATION   **6/8 Redcliffe Hill**

BATH HILL GARAGES   HIRE CARS
(Proprietor: S. W. Bouch)   Telephone: Day 76738 Night 77909

CARS BOUGHT, SOLD AND EXCHANGED   AUTOMOBILE ENGINEERS
REBORE SPECIALISTS   HIRE PURCHASE   INSURANCE

Local business advertisements from *Brislington Parish Magazine*, 1952. 'The Black Cat' on Bristol Hill was attached to the Ritz Cinema and is still fondly remembered. Bath Hill Garage (now Brislington Motor Services Ltd) is still run by the Bouch family today.

Cub Scouters at Beaver Lodge, 249th Eastwinds HQ at Nightingale Valley, 1953. Back row, from left to right: John Leece, Bill McDowell, Mike Comber (district Cub master), Bob Thomas. Front row: Diane Hartoe, Sheila Comber (Cub mistress).

St Cuthbert's Cubs' and Scouts' outing to Pensford departing from Brislington Station in the 1950s. Robertson's Jam Factory is on the left. Brislington Station opened on the Bristol & North Somerset line to Radstock on 3 September 1873. It was closed to passengers on 31 October 1959 and to freight on 7 October 1963. The line closed completely on 10 July 1968.

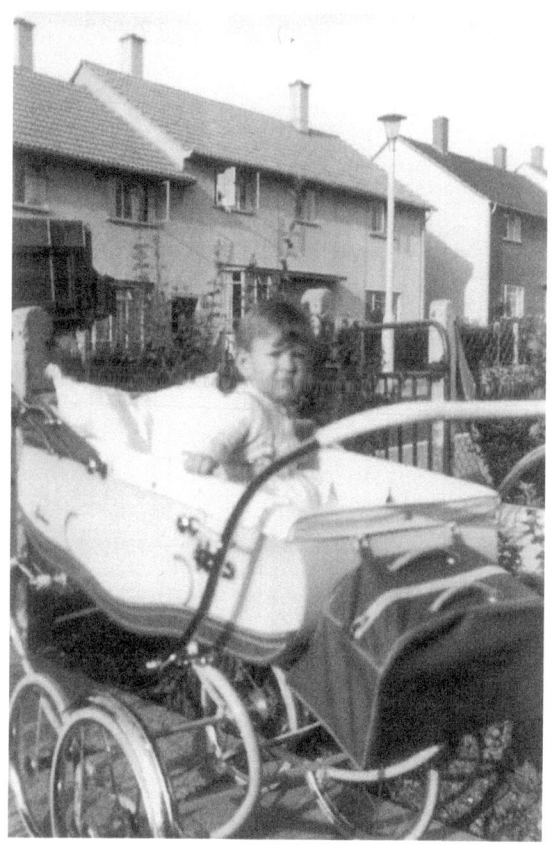

Left: Jonathan David Rowe aged ten months in his pram in the garden of No. 18 Hungerford Crescent, summer 1959.

Below: Brislington School in Hungerford Road which opened Easter 1956 and was officially opened by Minister of Education, the Rt Hon. Sir David Eccles MP, on 26 October 1956. Built on a site of 64 acres, the technical block was added in 1959, followed by the new main block in 1966 and the sports hall in 1968. The school was officially designated a comprehensive in 1962 and was one of the largest in the country. Renamed Brislington Enterprise College in 2004, the original buildings are being demolished for a new school on the same campus, which is due to open in 2008.

Class at West Town Lane Junior School, c. 1959.

West Town Lane Junior School, officially opened by Sir David Eccles MP on 26 October 1956. This building (originally the infants) was opened to pupils in September 1954 and was built on the site of West Town Farm. Stone from the demolished farmhouse was incorporated into the entrance wall seen on the left. A new infant school was built to the left in 1958. The schools were combined in 2006.

Farewell presentation to Revd Ivan Page-Wood (Vicar of St Cuthbert's 1950–1957), seen with his wife Norah, and Jennifer, one of his daughters, February 1957, at the Ruskin Hall in Wick Road. The presentation was made by Sid Spiers, and those present include: Jean and Bob Thomas, Maidie Kembery, Jeff Groves, Ruth and Roger Vaughan, Doug Locke, Fred Lewis, Graham Burgess, Roy Marsh, Mr Maynard, Mr Harding and Dinah Silcox.

Pilgrimage procession in Langton Court Road, *c.* 1959. The tradition of a pilgrimage and service at St Anne's Well was begun in 1927 by Revd C.F. Harman (Vicar of St Anne's Church 1927–1935) and was held over many years on or around St Anne's Day, 26 July. The Holy Well and Chapel of St Anne-in-the-Wood was founded around 1276 and became the third most important place of pilgrimage in medieval England until it was dissolved during the Reformation in 1538.

Flooding in The Square, Brislington village, 25 June 1959. The famous 'Great Flood' was to come nine years later, and the last time the village was badly flooded was in 1997. Williams & Stone builder's yard can be seen on the far left.

Sid Clark (right) supervising the shaping of brake lining at the Trist-Draper Top Dog factory on Bath Road in the 1950s. The material was shaped into a curve seen in the foreground, before being cut to size. The factory closed in 1985 after fifty-five years and was demolished for the B&Q store (now Toys R Us). In 1986 former employees of the defunct Trist Draper/Top Dog/Don Mintex founded a new company, EFI, with a workforce of five, which later moved to premises on the Bonville Trading Estate in Brislington.

Left: Residents in the garden of Uganda House (West Town House) elderly people's home in West Town Park, April 1952. Standing, left to right: Mr Breadman, Miss Howell (nurse). Seated, left to right: Miss Moore, Miss Parsons, Mrs Barrow. West Town House, parts of which date from around 1600, was an elderly people's home run by Bristol City Council from 1942–1953. It then became a boarding house before being converted into two private houses in 1962. The rear half became an elderly people's home in the 1980s, later becoming a home for mentally-handicapped people, which also took over the front half of the building in 2002.

Below: Fancy-dress parade at a garden party at Wick House children's home in the early 1950s. Annual fund-raising garden parties were held regularly throughout the 1950s. Wick House closed as a children's home in 1981 after fifty-six years. Note the 'Quality Street' couple on the left and the 'Bisto kids' on the right. Lynda Harris is the 'Nippy' waitress in the centre.

6

THE SWINGING SIXTIES
1960–1969

Arthur Heal delivering milk, Allison Road, Winter 1963.

The 1960s in Brislington got off to a swinging start with the opening of Arno's Court – the Georgian mansion and former Roman Catholic convent – as a hotel and nightclub. Arno's Court County Club opened in December 1960 and soon became a celebrated nightspot of the period with many stars of the day appearing there in cabaret. These included Matt Monro, Dusty Springfield, Adam Faith, Helen Shapiro, Morecambe and Wise, David Whitfield and Dickie Valentine. In 1965 a casino was added, the opening night being graced by the presence of the infamous Mandy Rice Davies, who was associated with those intimately connected with the Profumo Affair of 1963, which led to the downfall of the Minister for War.

In November 1960 the TWW (Television Wales and West) studios (now ITV West) opened next door to Arno's Court. The first major broadcast from the £25,000 television centre was a variety spectacular, *First Night*, which starred veteran comedian Bud Flanagan, singers Rosemary Squires and Ivor Emmanuel, pianist Joseph Cooper, with pop star of the day Marty Wilde topping the bill. TWW soon had its own teenage pop show, *Discs a Go Go*, which was advertised as being broadcast from 'The Gayest Coffee Bar in Town'. The Beatles made their second live television appearance on the programme in December 1962, miming to *Love Me Do*. The television franchise for Wales and West was taken over by Harlech TV (later HTV West) in May 1968, the launch being somewhat overshadowed by the appearance of shareholders Elizabeth Taylor and Richard Burton. This was the first public sighting of the famous 33-carat Krupp diamond ring which Burton had recently bought for £127,000, thus making the event worldwide headline news.

On a sadder note Brislington Railway Station closed in 1963 after ninety years and the line itself closed five years later. Industry also began to decline in Brislington with the closing of Terrells Rope Works (1965) and Smiths Crisps (1966), whose building was taken over by Radio Rentals (Rediffusion) in 1967. The distinctive period architecture of the building remained until the last part was demolished in the late 1980s.

1968 will always be remembered as the year of the Great Flood which affected much of the West Country that summer, when Brislington Brook broke its banks after 4in of rain fell in twelve hours on the evening of 10 July. Eighteen passengers on the No. 339 Bristol to Bath bus were marooned in 7ft water in Brislington Village and were eventually rescued by boat just after midnight. A week later the much loved and fondly remembered Ritz Cinema ended its short life of only thirty years.

Housing development continued all over Brislington and in 1964 Castlegate House, the first ten-storey block of flats in the area, was built in School Road. Late in 1968 work began on the demolition and redevelopment of the village with the removal of the wall of Brislington Hill House, whose attractive 'Gothic Lodge' at the top of the hill had gone two years earlier. Within a year, new shops and another tower block of flats, Gilton House, were rising on the skyline, and the heart of the old village was to set to disappear for ever.

Mary Backwell, a well-known face in the canteen at John Wright & Sons, the printing firm on Bath Road, in the 1960s. Mary worked at Wright's for many years and is seen here as a member of that fast-disappearing tradition – the 'Great British Tea Lady!'

The keyboard room at John Wright's in the 1960s. The factory was the first post-war development on Brislington Trading Estate and opened in 1948. Founded in 1825, the firm was one of Bristol's oldest printers and had a high reputation, particularly for its medical books.

Fred Stock, foreman of the monotype casting department at John Wright's, casting type for hymn sheets in the 1960s. The company closed in 1986 and the building was demolished for a McDonald's restaurant in 1992.

Hollywood Road, 1968. A view not greatly changed today, although the Old Poole's Yard development was built off right in 2004. This is one of Brislington's oldest roads, formerly called King's Arms Lane, and later Grove Road; it became Hollywood Road in the late 1920s.

The ruins of The Lindens in Church Hill, 1969. Little is known of this house which was believed to date from the early Victorian period. Linden trees formed arches in front of the house, hence the name. It became derelict after it was last occupied in the late 1950s and was demolished for Nos 35–39A Church Hill in 1969.

Anne Clark presents a bouquet to Mrs Monica Harrison, wife of the Rt Revd Douglas Harrison, Dean of Bristol, at the opening of the new St Luke's Church Hall in Church Parade on 18 January 1964.

Revd W.H. Osmund Moss and family, 1966. Revd Moss was Vicar of St Luke's 1955–1966, and is seen with his wife, Helen, youngest son Simon, and elder children Mary, Timothy and Michael.

The King's Arms at the junction of Bath Road and Hollywood Road, 1968. Traditionally believed to be Brislington's oldest pub, it is thought to date from the seventeenth century and landlords can be traced back to the 1780s.

The King's Arms on 11 July 1968, the day after the Great Flood. Landlord George O'Brien and barmaid Mrs E. Rudge are seen clearing up after flood water which was 5ft deep in the bar. A coin placed in the wall of the bar marks the level the water reached.

Church Hill Cottages, 1968. These cottages at the top of Church Hill are believed to date from around 1690–1700 and still stand today, although both have been drastically modernised.

William Stowell (1881–1969) in the kitchen of No. 2 Church Hill Cottages in the 1960s. William and his wife Ellen lived in the house from 1906–1970.

Mrs Ellen Stowell (1880–1970) in the kitchen of No. 2 Church Hill Cottages in the 1960s. Note the Victorian kitchen range on the left. Although this picture and that of Mr Stowell (*left*) were taken in the 1960s, their clothing and the appearance of the kitchen and its equipment could easily belong to a period several decades earlier.

Kingsley House, Brislington School class, 1961. The teacher at the front centre is Mr Symons.

Brislington School prefects, 1964. John Hellier, first headmaster 1955–1978, is in the front row, centre, with Miss Gilmore, senior mistress and Mr Buck, deputy head.

Local 'post Teddy Boys' outside Brislington Post Office in The Square, 24 March 1963. Left to right: Philip Anstey, Ron Alexander, Arnold Bennett, Bob Greenwood, John Anstey and Ivor Rudge. Forsey's butchers shop is on the left with Hollywood Road in the distance.

The Square, Brislington Village, 1968. Albert House on the right became the post office in 1896 but was demolished in 1971 along with the adjoining shops and Brislington Methodist Chapel, which was built in 1885 and closed in 1967. Woodland House on the far left was converted to flats in 1983.

Tarr's ice-cream van at the junction of Sandbach Road and Sandholme Road in the early 1960s. Colin Tarr can be seen serving from the van and the little boy by the lamp post is his son, Michael. Colin's father, Alfred Tarr, began the ice-cream business in 1920 at No. 14 Albert Crescent, St Philip's Marsh, where there was no electricity so all the ice cream was churned by hand. He began the business pushing a barrow with ice cream and served workmen building the St Anne's Park estate in the late 1920s. After a couple of years he progressed to a pony and cart and travelled as far as Yate market every Tuesday, which continued until the 1960s when the market closed. The business moved to No. 2 Sandown Road (formerly G.S Morris & Son, dairy) in 1946. Ice cream was sold as far out as Sturminster Road and Stockwood, which was then just beginning to be built.

Customers would buy ice cream in ½-litre blocks wrapped in paper to take home and eat immediately as refrigeration in the home was rare. Originally No. 2 Sandown Road was only used to manufacture ice cream but was later opened as a sweet shop as well.

The Tarr family also ran a stall at Severn Beach, the Pagoda Milk Bar, and had a pitch beside the Blue Lagoon for forty years. With the entry of Bradley Tarr, four generations of the family have now worked in the business and Tarr's vans travel as far as Plymouth, Guildford, Salisbury and Swansea. The ice cream sold today is basically the same recipe as the original one. There are also sixteen different sorts of ice lolly. Colin Tarr won the national championship cup for his ice cream in 1978 and has won it twelve times since then.

Opposite above: Junction of Sandown Road and Sandringham Road during the 'Hard Winter' of 1963. The snow shifted from footpaths was piled up as high as the roof of the mini van and did not melt for several weeks. The snow on the roofs slid down in one piece, hanging over the edge of the tiles until it fell or was knocked down by householders with brooms leaning from the bedroom windows. The guttering became so heavy with the weight of the snow and ice that the metal brackets began to give way. A group of neighbours equipped with ladders took down the guttering on several houses before it fell.

The cast of the historical pageant, *No Hands But Yours*, written by Joyce Allan, wife of Revd Ashford Allan (Vicar of St Luke's 1967–1976), which was performed in St Luke's Church in February 1969. The pageant told the story of Brislington from 1340 to 1968 and was produced for the organ and vestry fund, the present organ being installed in 1973.

Talbot Road Bridge, 1969. Thiery Road is off left. Eagle Cottage (originally Victoria House) on the far left, was built around 1870 and still stands today with its coach house and stables seen in the centre.

Water Lane, 1969. The gates on the left led to Robertson's Sports Ground where the Homemead Drive houses were built around 1985.

Right: Wick Cottage, The Rock, 1969. One of many picturesque cottages demolished in the early 1970s. The Rock is one of Brislington's oldest inhabited areas and was once a quarry, stone from which is said to have been used to build St Mary Redcliffe Church in Bristol.

Below: Sunnybank Cottage and Rock House, The Rock, 1969. From the mid-nineteenth century The Rock was owned by the Coggins family who ran a market garden here for 100 years from the 1860s. These cottages were demolished in the early 1970s for Millbank Close.

Oakenhill Cottages, off Bonville Road in the 1960s. Formerly part of the Clayfield-Ireland estate, these seventeenth/eighteenth-century tied cottages were let to agricultural labourers and still stand today alongside Oakenhill Farm, off left.

Gothic Cottage, off Church Hill, 1968. This group of cottages (there were originally three) are believed to date from the 1730s and became part of the Cooke-Hurle estate. They were bought in the 1930s by Jim Crabb who built an egg-packing plant nearby and lived in No. 3 Gothic Cottages until a new bungalow was built in approximately 1965 on the site of the other two cottages.

Brislington Football Club at Victory Park, c. 1960. The original Brislington Football Club was formed in 1887 and played in the grounds of Brislington House. From the turn of the century to the 1930s there were several teams in Brislington, including Brislington United, Brislington Athletic and Brislington Old Boys. All the local churches and chapels also had their own teams and sports grounds.

The present club was formed in 1957 by Alan (Joc) Parsons of Repton Road, who tragically died from chronic asthma aged only nineteen in 1961. The Alan Parsons Memorial Trophy is presented each year to the 'Clubman of the Year'. The club first played on a pitch at Arno's Park and played their first match against Holy Nativity in the junior section of the Church of England League on 7 September 1957. The original team, aged thirteen to fifteen, played in an old set of Bristol Rovers training kit donated by former Bristol Rovers player Ray Mabbutt, who lived opposite Arno's Park. Old tin baths from the backyard of Alan Parsons' home in Repton Road were donated and carried to the primitive dressing rooms (barns, previously occupied by sheep!) at the park for the players to wash after the game. Permission to set up the pitch was obtained from Bristol City Parks Dept. after pressure from Alan Parsons, first manager Charlie Hunt and local councillor Tom Martin. Among the early team members were Chris Rich, Mike Brewer, Gordon Barraclough, Glen Saunders, Bill Smith, Cedric Parker, Les Winterson, Andy Britton, John Harvey, Plummer Hardwick, Bonny Phillips and Alan Madge. Originally members only qualified to play for Brislington if they lived within a quarter-of-a-mile from Tarr's ice-cream shop in Sandown Road.

Bill Parsons took over the running of the club after his son's death and in 1960 they moved to a new pitch at Victory Park in School Road. In 1978 the club moved to their present ground in Ironmould Lane, where they shared facilities with Brislington Cricket Club until the present club house was built in 1984.

St Cuthbert's Cub Scouts playing football on 'The Paddock', alongside the TWW studios (now ITV West) on Bath Road in the early 1960s. The area is now a car park for the television studios. Terrell's Rope Works on the right closed in 1965 and was demolished. A Burger King restaurant was built on the site in 1994.

St Luke's 5th Bristol Scouts seen in West Town Lane during the St George's Day Parade, April 1964. The Rowan Walk prefabs were built by German Prisoners of War in 1945 and were demolished around 1974 for the Turnberry Walk houses.

Left: Alderman Tom Martin and Mrs Lorna Martin, Lord Mayor and Lady Mayoress of Bristol, 1965–1966. A tailor by trade, Alderman Martin was a well-known Labour city councillor for Brislington for over twenty-five years and lived in Harrow Road.

Below: Pilgrimage to St Anne's Well in St Anne's Woods in the 1960s. All local churches took part in the annual procession and open-air service which was held from 1927 until 1975, when the woods were deemed unsafe because of Dutch Elm Disease. The tradition was revived in 1986 and the last pilgrimage service was held in 2005. Revd J.E.M. Drummond (Vicar of St Anne's, 1956–1969) can be seen in the centre.

Quality Still Stands Supreme   Telephone 7-6893

BLAKES BAKERIES LIMITED
BRISLINGTON & KNOWLE

Head Office:
453 BATH ROAD, BRISTOL 4

Awarded over 2,000 Prizes
for Bread and Confectionery

REYNOLDS BROS.
FOR YOUR GROCERIES AND PROVISIONS

THE SQUARE, BRISLINGTON

Telephone No. 7-8949

"It's a Pleasure to Shop at Reynolds"

YOUR FIGURE PROBLEMS SOLVED

FREE CONSULTATIONS in the privacy of your home by a Registered SPENCER CORSETIERE

Consult :— Mrs. MUNFORD,
27 CALLINGTON ROAD,
BRISLINGTON, BRISTOL, 4

W. M. HOBBS   Telephone No. 7-8974
CONFECTIONER - NEWSAGENT - TOBACCONIST - LIBRARY
SIRDAR WOOLS   Speciality : PURE ICE-CREAM
4 WEST TOWN LANE, BRISLINGTON

KENSINGTON HAIR FASHIONS
LADIES' HAIRDRESSING
TINTING — RE-STYLING — PERMANENT WAVING
163 WINCHESTER ROAD, BRISTOL, 4
Telephone No. 7-6400

D. OSBORNE	R. A. REDMAN
8 THE SQUARE, BRISLINGTON	GROCERY & GREENGROCERY
FOOTWEAR REPAIRS	★
BEST MATERIALS	2 GROVE PARK ROAD.
Good Workmanship — at a Fair Price	BRISLINGTON, 4.

Left: Local advertisements from *Brislington Parish Magazine*, 1960. Out of the seven businesses seen here, only the newsagents and tobacconists in West Town Lane, run by the Hobbs family for two generations from the 1930s to the 1980s, is still trading today as Jai News.

Below: Gilton House flats and Merryweathers elderly people's flats on Brislington Hill being built in 1969. Church Hill House can be seen in centre distance.

7

RECESSION AND REDEVELOPMENT 1970 TO THE PRESENT DAY

View from Hollywood Road, 1990.

In the summer of 1970, the Brislington Hill footbridge and new shops were finally completed. Crowds watched as the last section of the bridge was swung into place during a long June evening. The following year the Georgian shops and post office, the Victorian Methodist chapel and an eighteenth-century house, Homeside, were demolished, leaving only a fraction of the old Brislington Square still standing. There was little interest in the demolition of the village and what replaced it, but when the once-familiar scene had gone forever, people began to realise with regret what Brislington had lost.

The last three decades have seen great changes in the area. The industrial and economic recession of the 1980s saw the closure of all of Brislington's well-known factories, beginning with St Anne's Board Mills, Robertson's Jam Factory and the CWS Clothing Factory (1980); Bristol Commercial Vehicles (1983); the 'Top Dog' works (1985); John Wright's the printers, the CWS Butter Factory (1986) and the CWS Dairy (1993). Today all these sites have been redeveloped into new businesses, housing and shops. Brislington Trading Estate is now mainly small independent units and car showrooms, although a few of the original 1930s buildings still survive. A McDonald's drive-in was opened on the site of the John Wright's building in 1992, and a Tesco supermarket was built on the Robertson's site in 1985. The Bristol Commercial Vehicles site on Kensington Hill was redeveloped into flats and retail units, including an MFI store which was officially opened by actress Helen Worth (*Coronation Street's* 'Gail Platt') in 1986.

Thousands watched as the 100ft landmark chimney of St Anne's Board Mills was demolished in 1984, and work began in 1992 to redevelop the site with shops, new housing and a satellite doctors' surgery. Several road names retain the area's historical links, such as Holywell Close, Pilgrim's Wharf, Langton Way, De La Warre Court (both names of families who were Lords of the Manor of Brislington) and Robertson Drive. Nearby Whitby Road, once dubbed 'Co-op Alley', is unrecognisable today as all the original industrial buildings were swept away in the 1990s. The Avonmeads shopping area was developed, incongruously, around the unique gothic folly, the 'Black Castle', which had first become a pub in 1978 then a family restaurant pub in 1995. Burger King, the Showcase Cinema and the Cargo Club store were opened in 1994, the latter becoming Sainsbury's two years later.

The Sutton housing estate off Wick Road, originally built in the 1920s, was demolished and rebuilt between 1992 and 2005. Two of Brislington's significant historic buildings have also seen major changes and a new lease of life. Brislington House, having been an asylum, a nurse's hostel and a nursing home, was restored and redeveloped into luxury flats in 2001. This bore a new name – Long Fox Manor – which retained the association with Dr Edward Long Fox, who founded the asylum in 1804. Wick House, once an attractive Georgian mansion, which had been a children's home and latterly an elderly people's nursing home, became a refugee hostel in 2003.

In 2006 a new £72 million Callington Road Hospital opened near Tesco. A Lidl store on the junction of Bath Road and West Town Lane finally opened nine years after the Crittalls windows factory had been demolished.

Brislington has changed beyond all recognition from the rural, country village of the late-Victorian period when the earliest of the photographs in this book were taken. A Brislington inhabitant returning to the village today would no doubt be shocked at the changes which have occurred over the last 130 years, but one thing that has survived is the community. Change is constant and even more rapid in today's world, but Brislington and its people survive and continue to thrive in the twenty-first century.

Construction of the footbridge over Brislington Hill, June 1970.

Brislington Hill footbridge completed, summer 1971. Jefferis newsagent's temporary shop stands on the left on the site of the former Methodist chapel, post office and shops which were demolished in April. 'Miss Millie's' takeaway and adjoining shops now occupy the site.

Brislington Hill, 1971. In recent years many of the shops have stood empty from time to time, but they now are being reoccupied.

Rose Villa, Talbot Road, *c.* 1985. This house is believed to date from around 1730. From 1937–1959 it was the home of Miss Martha and Miss Beatrice Wise, who moved from Hemplow House just across the road which had been the Wise family home since 1899. Rose Villa became an elderly people's home in 1985.

Rear view of Kensington House *c.* 1970, Bath Road, demolished in 1973 to build the PDSA hospital. Dating from around 1810, the grounds originally took in all of what is now the Kensington Park and Hampstead Road area. In the 1840s it became the home of Richard Jenkins Poole-King, a Bristol shipping merchant and Mayor of Bristol 1844–1845, whose name is perpetuated in King's Road. Kensington House was used as the clubhouse for St Christopher's Church, a tank regiment during the Second World War, the Territorial Army and finally a greetings-cards firm. The coach house and stables still stand and are used by Army and Air Force cadets.

The Woodlands, West Town Lane, c. 1970. Dating from around 1750, the building was formerly known as Woodbridge House and was once one of only seven houses in a leafy country lane until modern housing development began in 1928. In 1938 The Woodlands was divided into two houses, as it is today.

Hill Cottage, Brislington Hill, c. 1970. Believed to date from around 1660, Hill Cottage became part of the Clayfield-Ireland estate and was occupied from approximately 1884–1924 by David Cox Sherwell, who was Sunday school superintendent of the Wesleyan Methodist Chapel in the village for many years. His name is perpetuated in Sherwell Road. The Mitchell family were occupants from 1926–1976, when the house became known for its distinctive trellis and colourful window boxes.

Sandy Park Gospel Hall at the junction of Sandholme Road and Upper Sandhurst Road, 1998. The original hall was built in 1908 and replaced the 'Tent Mission' where meetings had been held from 1905. An extension was added in 1918 and a new hall was built in 1921. The Gospel Hall was closed and redeveloped for housing in 1998.

St Anne's Park Brotherhood and Sisterhood building, Wick Road, 2006. Built in 1927, it became the Disabled Christian Fellowship in 1990 and was demolished for flats in 2006.

Arno's Vale Cemetery, Bath Road, 2007. Opened in 1836 by Bristol Cemetery Co. at a cost of £13,340, the first eight acres were consecrated by Revd Dr Monk, Bishop of Gloucester and Bristol, on 27 October 1840. *Felix Farley's Bristol Journal* quotes:

> The beauty of the morning attracted a large concourse of spectators including our resident fashionables ... we think we may with all safety predict when all the arrangements are completed, the grounds planted, the various tombs and monuments erected, few, if any cemeteries in the kingdom will surpass that of Bristol.

The eighteenth-century Arno's Vale House previously stood here in grounds covering forty acres. The house was demolished in 1837 and the site was considered for Bristol Zoo, which was being planned at the time. By the end of the nineteenth century 96,000 burials had taken place.

Over 140 years the cemetery had become overgrown and uncared for, when it was bought by Mr Tony Towner in 1985. After public opposition to Mr Towner's plans for redevelopment of the site, the Association for the Preservation of Arno's Vale Cemetery (APAC) was set up, becoming Friends of Arno's Vale in 1998. In 2003 Bristol City Council bought the land under compulsory purchase order and Arno's Vale Cemetery Trust was established to restore the site. They succeeded in obtaining a grant of £4.8 million Heritage Lottery funding in 2005. The Non-Conformist chapel is in the centre and the monument on the right commemorates the celebrated Indian social reformer and philanthropist Raja Rammohun Roy (1772–1833). Restoration work is now in progress and will include a family history research centre, based in one of the lodges at the entrance to the cemetery.

Gravestone in St Luke's churchyard commemorating Catherine Anne Hubbuck (1818–1877), daughter of Sir Francis William Austen, Admiral of the Fleet, and a niece of writer Jane Austen (1775–1817). Catherine Anne Austen married John Hubbuck in 1842 and they had four children. They lived at Malvern, then in Wales, and later at Birkenhead. John Hubbuck was a promising young lawyer but tragically, in 1847, intense overwork brought on a complete mental breakdown. To distract herself from perpetual anxiety, and in the hope of earning money now that her husband's income had ended, Catherine rewrote a version of Jane Austen's unfinished novel *The Watsons*, which was published in 1850 as *The Younger Sister*. It was dedicated to the memory of Jane Austen by the authoress who 'Though too young to have known her personally, was from early childhood taught to esteem her virtues and admire her talents'. In May 1850 John Hubbuck was confined to Brislington House Asylum, where he lived until his death in February 1885. Catherine went on to publish ten books between 1850 and 1863, and became a minor female Victorian novelist, much admired by 'middle-class young ladies', among them the grandmother of American writer Henry James.

Catherine was a most ardent, spirited and imaginative woman – 'vivid' was how her son described her personality. In 1871 at the age of fifty-three, she went to America where her son John had emigrated and had become a prosperous grain merchant. She died at the home of her third son, Charley, who had also emigrated to America, while visiting him on his smallholding in Virginia on 27 February 1877. The grave is situated opposite the west door of St Luke's.

Left: Revd Peter Dyson, December 1990, priest in charge of St Luke's Church, 1984–1991. A very popular parish priest, he led the successful Tower and Bells Restoration Appeal of 1987–1988 and founded St Luke's Church Players in 1988.

Below: Pilgrimage service at St Anne's Well, St Anne's Woods, 26 July 1986, led by Revd Mark Waters (Vicar of St Anne's Church, 1985–1991). The domed canopy was added to the well in 1927 but by the 1990s had become dilapidated and was removed. The well was restored by the Source group in 1995 and a statue of St Anne was erected, but sadly the work was vandalised soon afterwards.

West Town Lane Railway Bridge, April 1974. Sturminster Road is off left. The bridge was demolished in 1978.

Brislington Station, 1990. The station stood off Talbot Road and the building became derelict after the station closed in 1963. The land around was used as a coal and scrap yard and the station buildings were eventually demolished in 1997. A Tesco store is off right.

Top of Fry's Hill, 1986. Leading from Bellevue Terrace to Hollywood Road this lane takes its name from William Fry, the earliest known occupant of The Grove, the late eighteenth-century house which stands at the top of Bristol Hill. The cottages at the top left date from the 1880s.

Fry's Hill, looking from Hollywood Road, 1986. This was a steep muddy path until these stone setts were laid by Brislington Parish Council in 1896. The cottages on the right are probably eighteenth or early nineteenth century. The wall on the left is the side of The Pilgrim public house which dates from around 1900 and replaced an earlier pub of the same name which was first established in about 1840.

Blagdon Lodge, Bristol Hill, 1984. Built around 1820, this house was originally known as Ivy Lodge and this name was visible on the entrance gate pillars seen here, until the recent demolition of the building. The pillars have now been replaced with modern replicas. The house was built by the Ricketts family who lived at The Grove and they continued to own the property until about 1900. From 1886–1890 this was the home of Revd John Lindsay, Resident Curate of St Luke's Church, and was known as St Luke's Lodge.

Garden front view of Blagdon Lodge, Bristol Hill, 1984. The house became known as Blagdon Lodge in the 1890s, and in 1904 it became the 'Derry Hand Laundry'. The house and business were taken over by James Galley in 1908 and the family continued the business until the 1950s. In 1959 the house was bought by Romeo Verrecchia, an ice-cream manufacturer who lived there, converting part of the house into flats. The family opened a new factory in Stockwood Lane and in 1960 launched the first ice-cream van in Bristol. The business closed in 1998 and Blagdon Lodge was demolished in 2006 to build Grove Park Court flats.

Heathcourt, Ironmould Lane, 1986. Formerly known as Heath Farm, Heathcourt dates from the seventeenth century with nineteenth-century additions. It was originally part of the estate of the Bridges family of Keynsham and passed to a descendant, Richard Plantagenet, second Duke of Buckingham and Chandos (1797–1861) who sold the property in about 1840 to Dr Francis Ker Fox and Dr Charles Joseph Fox of Brislington House Asylum. It then became the Home Farm for the Brislington House estate, supplying the asylum and the Fox family with milk, butter, eggs and other farm produce.

In the nineteenth and early twentieth century Heath Farm was occupied by the farm bailiff of Brislington House, often with patients from the asylum also living in part of the house. In about 1920 the house appears to have been divided and was known as Heath Cottage and Heath Farm Villa, being occupied by the farm bailiff and later the chauffeur to the Fox family.

After Brislington House Asylum closed in 1952 and the estate was broken up, Heath Farm was bought by John Reynolds of Reynolds Brothers Dairy, who lived there from about 1950 until 1978 and ran a plant nursery. The nursery business was operated by Alan Cook from 1973 to 1998. In 1978 the front part of the building was opened as Heathcourt Restaurant by Lord and Lady Cadman. The business was taken over by Tony and Claire Groves in 1992 and closed in 2000 when the building became a private house again.

Oakenhill Farm, off Bonville Road, 2006. This is believed to be Brislington's oldest surviving farmhouse, dating from the late sixteenth century. The front door on the right originally faced the route of the old Bath Road. Oakenhill Farm became part of the Clayfield-Ireland estate in about 1794 when it was purchased by James Ireland of Brislington Hall (1724–1814). From around 1900 the farm was let to Ted Brean of Woodbine Farm in Water Lane, who left the farmhouse unoccupied. He left when the Clayfield-Ireland estate was being broken up in the 1920s after the death of the last 'Squire of Brislington', Alfred Clayfield-Ireland (1851–1923). The property was inherited along with the rest of the estate by Lt-Col James St George Priaulx Armstrong (1874–1939) and after his death was run by the Armstrong Trust.

The farmhouse was then let separately, the farm itself being run by the Carey family (Harry and his son Gordon) from around 1928 until about 1950. The farm included cows, calves, sows and chickens, and the Careys ran a dairy round in the village selling milk and eggs. The farm cowsheds can still be seen today. The milk round finished in about 1947 when the farmhouse (later bought by Bristol City Council and then resold) was let to the Smith family, who still live there today. The farmhouse has been renovated in recent years and a modern house has been built on the left.

The Radio Rentals building, Bath Road, decorated for the visit of Queen Elizabeth II during the 'Bristol 600' celebrations, 6 August 1973. Built as Smith's Crisps factory in 1936, it became Radio Rentals in 1966 and was partially demolished in 1988. In 1995 the site at the junction of Bath Road and Stockwood Lane was redeveloped as a car showroom.

Crittall's Windows building, Bath Road, September 1995. Seen shortly after it closed down, this was the first factory to be built in 1927 on what was to become Brislington Trading Estate.

The building was demolished in 1997, and the distinctive Art Deco doors were removed to an architectural museum in Braintree, Essex. The Lidl store was built on the site in 2006.

Right: HTV Studios, Bath Road, 1992. Originally opened as TWW in November 1960. Harlech TV (later HTV West) took over the franchise in 1968 until 2004, when it became ITV West. A £3 million extension to the building was opened by Princess Anne in 1986.

Below: The John Peer furniture building, Bath Road in the 1980s. This was formerly the CWS Clothing Factory built in 1936 on the site of Kensington Place, a terrace of three houses built around 1795 which became the original CWS factory in 1920. The factory closed in 1980 and was taken over by John Peer in 1986, but since this business closed the building has been left vacant.

Jonathan Rowe outside The Brislington Cinema, Sandy Park Road, 31 July 1991, holding the programme card for the cinema's final week in 1956. This was Brislington's first silent cinema, and was one of the earliest purpose-built 'picture houses' in Bristol. It opened in 1913 and was originally known for about two years as 'The Empress'. It was initially run by Ralph Pringle of Pringle's Pictures (North American Animated Picture Co.) and was taken over by Harry Miall Tomkins in about 1919.

Mr Tomkins also ran Bristol Film Services Ltd, a film distribution service at No. 127 Victoria Street, Bristol in the 1920s. The first screen was a blank wall, later replaced by a screen of perforated rubber. Harry Tomkins' son, George, took over the cinema in the early 1930s. It was one of the last cinemas in Bristol to be converted to 'talking pictures' in 1931. A sign outside the cinema read 'Silence Is Golden', which was eventually converted to 'Until Our Screen Speaks'.

In 1938 The Brislington was extended by taking over a corn merchant next door, and a balcony and new entrance were built. This was done to compete with the new and ultra-modern Ritz Cinema built at the junction of Bristol Hill and Warrington Road, which opened in October of the same year.

The Brislington survived the introduction of the 'talkies', the Depression and two world wars, but increasing competition from television and more up-to-date cinemas saw audiences decline and it finally closed on 29 December 1956. The last films to be screened were *Jeopardy* starring Barbara Stanwyck and *The Long, Long Trailer* starring Lucille Ball and Desi Arnaz. The building remained empty until it was bought by Denys Chamberlain of the well-known cinema family who owned several Bristol cinemas including the Gaiety, the Knowle and the Broadway. The Chamberlains opened it as the Brislington Bingo Club in 1962, which continued until the 1990s when it closed and was later converted into 'Kinema House' flats by United Housing Association.

Brislington Conservation and Amenity Society's 'Victorian Brislington' exhibition at St Cuthbert's Church Crypt, Sandy Park Road, 19 September 1992. Society members portrayed real Brislington people in the late-Victorian period. From left to right: Pat Sweet as Susan Coggins, market gardener of The Rock; Judith Chard as Mrs Florence Anne Cooke-Hurle of Brislington Hill House; Jonathan Rowe as John Royle Williams, first station master of Brislington Station; and Toby Hayers (*crouching*) as Bert Stowell, stable lad of Oakenhill Cottages.

The society has held several day exhibitions of photographs, maps, books and memorabilia illustrating various aspects of Brislington's local history. The first of these was *Brislington at War* (1989) which marked the 50th anniversary of the outbreak of the Second World War. This was followed by *Brislington in the Twenties and Thirties* (1990), *Briz Before the War* (1993), *Brislington and the Great War* (1994), which commemorated the eighty years since the outbreak of the First World War and *50th Anniversary of VE Day* (1995). The 1996 exhibition was 'Braikenridge and Brislington', which gave people an insight into the life and times of George Weare Braikenridge of Broomwell House, which stood in Wick Road. A local landowner, merchant and antiquarian, in the 1820s he commissioned a collection of drawings of Brislington and Bristol, the majority of which are now in the Bristol City Museum & Art Gallery.

Broomhill Co-op supermarket at the junction of Broomhill Road and Fermaine Avenue, 1991. This was Brislington's first supermarket, opened in December 1958 and still trading today.

St Peter's Methodist Church, Allison Road, 2008. Opened on 11 December 1971, this church replaced an older building dating from 1952 on the same site.

The Good Intent, Broomhill Road, 2008. The pub was opened on 9 April 1939 on the birthday of the first landlord, William Entwhistle. After he left in 1940, Mr Entwhistle, his wife Evelyn and daughter Joan ran the King's Arms in Brislington Village from 1941–1964.

Birchwood Road prefabs at Broomhill, 2008. The prefabs were built in 1945 as temporary housing for people made homeless by the Second World War. This picture was taken shortly before their demolition for redevelopment of the site.

Above: Eastwood Farm, off Wyndham Crescent, Broomhill, 2004. This seventeenth-century Grade II Listed farmhouse has fine moulded-plaster ceilings, a carved-stone fireplace and a carved, oak staircase. It was part of the Clayfield-Ireland estate from 1774, and was later owned by the Armstrong Trust until 1959. It was the last working dairy farm in Brislington. Arthur Heal (1900–1993) was the last farmer to live there from 1928–1959 and last dairyman in Brislington continuing his milk round until 1981. For much of the time the Heal family lived here, there was no electricity or running water.

Left: Moulded-plaster ceiling plaque at Eastwood Farm depicting St Peter holding the keys of heaven with vine motifs. The plaque, which is believed to weigh nearly ½cwt, is said to be close in character to work in the contemporary 'Llandoger Trow' pub in King Street, Bristol.

Gravestone of Thomas Newman in St Luke's churchyard, 2008. The deeply incised Inscription reads: '1542 Thomas Newman aged 153. This stone was new faced in the year 1771 to perpetuate the great age of the deceased'. Was Thomas Newman really the oldest man ever to live in this country? Revd Alfred Richardson (Vicar of St Luke's, 1890–1902), wrote: 'Possibly he (Newman) did live to be 103 and when the stone was refaced there was a difficulty in telling whether the middle figure was "0" or "5", and the carver gave "5" the benefit of the doubt'. But is it all a fake? Revd John Collinson wrote in his *History and Antiquities of the County of Somerset* (1791): 'The original numerals on this tomb were simply 53, but some arch wag, by prefixing the figure 1, made the person interred one year older than the celebrated Thomas Parr, who died in 1625 aged 152'.

James Bowden, a descendant of Thomas Newman, told Dr Charles Fox on 10 January 1853: 'The grandmother of James Bowden was a Miss Anne Newman, who was a lineal descendant of Thomas Newman of great age, buried in Brislington Churchyard, and she stated to James Bowden that the tombstone of the said Thomas Newman was resurfaced by the executors of her father'. The Newmans had property in Brislington and at one time owned the White Hart. To further add to the confusion there is also a board in the belfry of Bridlington Priory, East Yorkshire, with a virtually similar inscription as the tombstone in Brislington saying the board is a copy of an inscription of 'an ancient stone in Bridlington churchyard which has now disappeared'. This came to light in 1984 when the editor of the parish magazine found an entry in the church visitor's book dating from 1970 by Stanley Spencer of Liverpool, another descendant of Thomas Newman. On making contact he stated that he had a copy of a framed record relating to the story of Thomas Newman and his great age, which maintained that Thomas Newman was also the Vicar of Brislington!

Imperial Rugby Team 1985–1986, Imperial Club Ground, West Town Lane. Back row, from left to right: Dave Walker, Mike Rogers, Alan Gibbard, Ian Williams, Rich Lewis, Joe Maniglia, Ken Bennett.

Second row: Terry Cockle, John Hearne, Andy Monks, John Hamburn, Kim Crocker, Phil Knight, Nigel Brookes. Front row: Andy Buckle, Tony Morris. The club, which is still active, began in 1906 when all players had to be employed by a company within the Imperial Group. The pavilion in the background was built in 1909 and housed Belgian refugees during the First World War. The pavilion burnt down in 1999 and the Hither Bath Bridge development now stands on the site.

The cast of St Luke's Church historical Brislington pageant, *All God's Children*, performed in St Luke's Church, March 1972. The play was written by Joyce Allan, wife of Revd Ashford Allan (Vicar of St Luke's, 1967–1976), who is seen in the agricultural labourer's smock on far right. Revd Austin Thomas, (Curate of St Luke's, 1968–1973), is seen in centre holding the cross, and Revd John Richardson, (Minister of St Peter's Methodist Church, 1969–1974) is fourth from the right.

Plaque at Keeper's Cottage, Brislington Hill, unveiled in 2002 commemorating the opening in 1796 of the first school for village children in Brislington by Bristol writer and philanthropist, Hannah More (1745–1833). The cottage, believed to date from around 1691, was formerly part of the Clayfield-Ireland estate. Hannah More was a friend of James Ireland of Brislington Hall (1724–1814), and wrote the epitaph on the memorial in St Luke's Church to his first wife, Frances Godde, who died in 1805.

The Christadelphian Hall, Church Hill, 2008. This was Brislington's first public meeting hall, opened on 7 October 1878 as the Band of Hope Assembly Rooms. Temperance, political and recruiting meetings (for Army, Navy and the colonies) were held here in Victorian and Edwardian times as well as magic-lantern shows and tea parties. During the Second World War it was used by St Luke's Church as a temporary hall after the Water Lane building was requisitioned, and in the 1950s it became an annexe for Hollywood Road School. It was taken over by the Christadelphian Church in the late 1960s.

Brislington War Memorial, Kensington Hill, Bath Road, 2008. Built by public subscription to commemorate Brislington men who died during the First World War, it was unveiled by Mrs Bonville Bradley Fox of Brislington House on 11 November 1922.

Opposite above: Archaeologist Andrew Young at the excavation site at the Hollybush public house at the junction of Kenneth Road and Bristol Hill. This dig excavated the site after the Hollybush was demolished in 2007 for the present Chapel Court flats. The photograph shows what could have been a cellar of the medieval building which stood on the site. Part of this building became the original Hollybush Inn around 1860 which was demolished in 1903 to build the Edwardian red-brick pub.

Opposite below: Excavations during the archaeological dig at the site of the Hollybush, 2007. Three trenches show the original boundary ditch. The site is said to have been a medieval pilgrim's hostelry for those on pilgrimage to St Anne's Chapel.

Entrance to Bristol Commercial Vehicles, Kensington Hill, shortly before closure in 1983. Originally opened in 1912 as the Motor Constructional Works by Bristol Tramways & Carriage Co., the works produced bus chassis and lorries which sold worldwide. In 1935 additional premises were opened at Chatsworth Road. The business was run by the Tilling group of bus manufacturers from 1935–1947, when it was nationalised. Subsequently becoming Bristol Commercial Vehicles (1955), then Leyland Motors (1965), the firm was closed in 1983. The site was redeveloped and the MFI and Great Mills stores were opened in 1986 with the Roman Walk flats being built on the left.

Opposite above: Demolition of Mardon Son & Hall, St Anne's Road, *c.* 1990. Founded in Bristol in 1823, Mardon's became one of the leading cardboard-carton manufacturers in Europe. Seven factories were built in the Temple and Redcliffe areas of Bristol, producing cigarette boxes for WD & HO Wills, tobacco manufacturers, before the St Anne's factory was opened in 1922 alongside St Anne's Board Mills. An adjoining factory was opened in 1962 before Mardon's was taken over and the factory closed in 1987. The firm trades today as 'Lawson Mardon' in Warmley.

Opposite below: Demolition of St Anne's Board Mills, St Anne's Road, *c.* 1984. St Anne's Board Mills opened in 1914 and eventually covered a 100-acre site. By 1958 100,000 tons of packaging a year was being produced by a workforce of 1,800. The mills finally closed in 1980 and in 1984 the last of the 100ft-high chimneys that had dominated the skyline for over sixty years was demolished. By 1992 the site had been cleared and work had begun on the present development of houses and shops which now cover the site.

The authors of *Brislington Revisited*, Graham Crimmins and Jonathan Rowe, Lynda Harris and Beth Knight, sitting on the ancient village preaching cross in St Luke's Churchyard. Augustinian canons from Keynsham Abbey preached to medieval Brislington villagers from the steps of this 18ft cross. Dating from at least the thirteenth century, it certainly predates the first record of the church in 1308. The earliest part of the church we see today was built in about 1420. Village tradition has it that the cross originally stood in Brislington Square and was moved to the churchyard at a later date. The ball at the top of the column was replaced by a cross in 1872 and this survived until it was destroyed by vandals about 100 years later, when it reverted to a stone ball as illustrated in an early drawing of the cross in the 1820s.

Other local titles published by The History Press

Brislington
JUDITH CHARD, MARY AXFORD MITCHELL AND JONATHAN ROWE

Published in 1995, this is the Brislington Conservation and History Society's first book on this intriguing village's past, and a must-read for fans of *Brislington Revisited* or those who have visited this area of Bristol. Containing more pictures and stories from Brislington's history, this is guaranteed to delight anyone with an interest in the village.

978 0 7524 0351 9

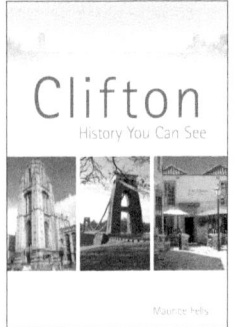

Clifton History You Can See
MAURICE FELLS

In this book the reader is taken on a delightful stroll around Clifton Village, visiting the church where Agatha Christie married one Christmas Eve, the railway through the rocks of Avon Gorge, Royal York Crescent, the Clifton Club, Watts Folly Clifton library, eighteenth-century Goldney House with its grotto made of sea shells, Clifton college, Brunel's Clifton Suspension Bridge plus lots more.

978 0 7524 4332 4

Barton Hill Revisited
BARTON HILL HISTORY GROUP

This second collection of over 200 previously unseen photographs takes a fresh look at Barton Hill. a lively comminuty in East Bristol. The area was redeveloped during the 1950s and 1960s and these images document the huge changes that took place at that time. Recalling such landmarks as Max Williams' much-loved toy shop, the swimming baths and the Barrow Road railway yard, this book will appeal to all who know the area.

978 0 7524 3557 2

Easton, Eastville and St Jude's
VERONICA SMITH

This revealing collection of over 200 images brings to life the people and places of this fascinating area of Bristol. From the corner shops that grew in abundance in the early part of the twentieth century to the many community groups who gathered together here, the reader is taken on a nostalgic journey around the district. *Easton, Eastville and St Judes* will delight long-term residents and newcomers alike.

978 0 7524 3712 5

If you are interested in purchasing other books published by The History Press, or in case you have difficulty finding any History Press books in your local bookshop, you can also place orders directly through our website

www.thehistorypress.co.uk